Friendly
WordPerfect

Friendly Computer Books are available for the following major software programs:

Friendly DOS
by The LeBlond Group
(ISBN 0-553-56214-2)

Friendly Excel 4.0 for Windows
by Jack Nimersheim
(ISBN 0-553-56215-0)

Friendly Quicken for Windows
by The LeBlond Group
(ISBN 0-553-56216-9)

Friendly Windows 3.1
by Kay Yarborough Nelson
(ISBN 0-553-56211-8)

Friendly Word for Windows 2.0
by Jack Nimersheim
(ISBN 0-553-56212-6)

Friendly WordPerfect
by Kay Yarborough Nelson
(ISBN 0-553-56213-4)

Friendly
WordPerfect

Kay Yarborough Nelson

BANTAM BOOKS
NEW YORK • TORONTO • LONDON • SYDNEY • AUCKLAND

Friendly WordPerfect
A Bantam Book / February 1993

ISBN 0-553-56213-4

Published simultaneously in the United States and Canada

Bantam Books are published by Bantam Books, a division of
Bantam Doubleday Dell Publishing Group, Inc. Its trademark,
consisting of the words "Bantam Books" and the portrayal of
a rooster, is Registered in U.S. Patent and Trademark Office
and in other countries. Marca Registrada, Bantam Books, 666
Fifth Avenue, New York, New York 10103.

PRINTED IN CANADA

0   9   8   7   6   5   4   3

Contents

14 Undoing More Mistakes 85

15 Searching and Replacing 89

16 The Speller 95

17 Working with Blocks of Text 103

18 Setting Document Margins 109

Preface

Most of us become computer users because we have to, because knowledge of a particular software package is needed for a job, or because computer-assisted productivity is essential to success in business. There are hundreds of reasons. Computers and software are only the means to an end. They have become a necessity of life, and this requirement shapes the way we go about learning how to use software.

Not everyone is interested in every detail of a particular program. Here is a quick, no-nonsense introduction that teaches the basic skills needed to use the software.

In approximately 200 pages, each Friendly Computer Book covers the basic features of a specific popular software in a way that will get new users up and running quickly. The result is a series of computer books that has these unifying characteristics:

- **Topic-oriented organization.** Short, self-contained lessons focus on a particular topic or area that is important in learning to use the software.

When you finish the lesson, you'll have mastered an aspect of the software.

- **Spacious layout.** Large type and a spacious layout make the books easy on the eyes and easy to use.
- **Step-by-step approach.** Numbered lists help you to concentrate on the practical steps needed to get your work done.
- **Numerous screen shots.** Each lesson contains at least two screen shots that show you exactly how your screen should look.
- **Frequent use of icons.** Many eye-catching icons—drawing attention to important aspects of the text and software—are placed throughout the book.
- **Lay-flat binding.** Friendly Computer Books stay open as you work.
- **And finally, a low, low price.**

For many users Friendly Computer Books are all they'll need. For others who want to learn more about the software, we've suggested further readings.

Enjoy the friendly approach of Friendly Computer Books!

Ron Petrusha
Series Editor

◆ *Lesson* ◆

1

Word Processing with WordPerfect

WordPerfect is the best-selling word processing program of all time. In fact, it's estimated that about ten million people use the program every day. Learning to use WordPerfect is a smart choice, because all of the other word processing programs accept WordPerfect documents; and there are versions of WordPerfect for many types of computers, including Apple, Macintosh, Atari, Data General, IBM/370, Amiga, and VAX. The DOS version of WordPerfect—which this book will teach you—is by far the most widely used, and it runs on any computer running DOS, from an IBM XT or clone to the fastest top-of-the-line machines on the market.

What makes WordPerfect so popular is that you can use it to do just about everything from writing a simple note to doing sophisticated desktop publishing with graphics. And, for a program with such an abundance of features, it's surprisingly easy to use.

WordPerfect DOS or WordPerfect Windows?

WordPerfect 5.1 is available in both DOS and Windows versions. The features in both of them are remarkably similar, and you can work with documents created in either one of them in the other. But to be perfectly frank, the DOS version is quite a bit faster because it's text-based. Therefore, processes like spell checking go very quickly. WordPerfect for Windows is a graphical program, on the other hand, and a certain amount of your computer's power has to go to drawing the graphics screen, which slows the program down. In addition, the Windows version runs only on the more top-of-the-line computers that have large memory capacities. So it's a wise choice to learn how to use the standard DOS version of the program, and then later switch to the Windows version, if you like.

What WordPerfect Can Do

If you do any kind of typing—and who doesn't—WordPerfect can make your work faster and easier.

Seeing your text on the screen helps you organize your thoughts better than scribbling notes on a sheet of paper. With WordPerfect, you can make changes quickly, and instantly see the results. And, if you need to reorganize or edit a document, that's easy, too. You can insert new text or delete blocks of text, and copy words and entire paragraphs without having to retype them from scratch. If you delete something and change your mind later, you can get it back: Word-

Perfect remembers the last *three* things you erased. You can search for a word or phrase and replace it with another, instantly, everywhere it appears in a document. Changing a document's formatting, such as resetting its margins and line spacing, requires only a couple of keystrokes. A built-in spell checker catches your typing mistakes. And you can use different typefaces and **bold** and *italic* type to give a sophisticated, published look to your documents.

Let's look at a few of the many practical things you can use WordPerfect to do.

- Write memos and notes, letters and magazine articles, make lists—even write entire books.
- Create newsletters and flyers that include graphics.
- Address envelopes and labels.
- Create tables and charts, such as a schedule of events or a class schedule.
- Create and fill out forms.
- Alphabetize lists, like name-and-address lists or student rolls.
- Type with foreign language characters and use special symbols.
- Create indexes, footnotes, and tables of contents.
- Assemble large documents from small ones.

More Than a Word Processing Program

But WordPerfect does much more than what's listed here. It gives you features that are far beyond the capabilities of a standard word processing program.

WORKS LIKE A DATABASE

WordPerfect, for example, can be used with records from a database program. Say that you have a huge list of names and addresses, and you need to address labels or envelopes for all of them. With WordPerfect, you can just set up a mail merge to do the job for you. It will insert information into form letters for you, too— the kind that say "Dear Mrs. Smith, You have just won ten million dollars."

WORDPERFECT DOES SPREADSHEETS, TOO

Spreadsheet capabilities are also built into Word-Perfect. It's easy to bring a spreadsheet created by one of the popular spreadsheet programs, like Lotus 1-2-3, Excel, or Quattro Pro, into the documents you create with WordPerfect, so you don't have to tediously re-type columns of data.

BUILT-IN EXTRAS

In addition to a great spell checker, WordPerfect also has a built-in thesaurus for when you need to find just the right alternate word. Another popular feature that many people use is macros. When the macro recorder is on, the program records what you type, so that you can play it back later just by pressing a couple of keys. This is the perfect solution for typing the same thing over and over.

UNLIMITED TOLL-FREE SUPPORT

One final thing that makes WordPerfect such a popular program is WordPerfect Corporation's policy of unlimited toll-free technical support. If you have a problem you can't solve, call the kind and incredibly patient folks at WordPerfect, who will talk you through it until you get it right. No other word processing program offers this service, which is legendary in its field. Write down or memorize this number: (800) 541-5096. There are many other 800 numbers for specialized Word-Perfect support, and some of them are listed in the last chapter of this book, but this one will get you to the main operator.

How to Use This Book

We won't cover all of WordPerfect's features in this book, or it would be a thousand pages long! But you're probably not interested in everything the program can do, at least not right now. Use this book to learn the basics and then explore the other parts as you need them, on your own.

WordPerfect isn't hard to master, especially when you approach it one lesson at a time. By working along with the step-by-step examples in this book, you'll be using WordPerfect in no time. Go at your own pace and stop when you get tired. Nobody's looking over your shoulder to see how you're doing. There are no tests, either.

This is how the step-by-step exercises are set up:

1. Anything you are instructed to type appears in **boldface**.

2. When two or more keys must be pressed at the same time, they are separated with a hyphen (-). For example, "press **Alt-F4**" means press the Alt key and the function key F4 on your keyboard at the same time.

Have fun! The first exercise shows you how to install the program on your computer, in case that hasn't already been done for you.

◆ *Lesson* ◆

2

Installing WordPerfect

If WordPerfect is already installed on your computer, you can skip this lesson. But if you're not sure, there's an easy way to tell. Start up your computer. Type **wp** when you see the C:\> symbol (the DOS prompt) and then press **Enter**. If WordPerfect appears, it's installed, and you can skip to Lesson 3.

If WordPerfect doesn't appear, your computer may have more than one hard disk drive, and you may be on the wrong one. Try typing **d:** and then press **Enter** at the DOS prompt to change to drive D. (If you see a message saying "invalid drive specification," you know that you don't have a drive D.) If the C:\> symbol changes to D:\>, type **wp** and press **Enter** again to see if WordPerfect is on that drive. If it doesn't come up then, it's probably not installed on your computer yet.

The Install Procedure

If you do need to install the program, follow these easy steps. And by all means, install it onto your hard drive.

Although it's possible to install WordPerfect onto floppy disks, it's not recommended.

1. Put the Install/Learn/Utilities 1 disk in your floppy disk drive. Use either the 5.25-inch disks or the 3.5-inch disks, depending on what type of disk drive you have.
2. The top or left-hand disk drive on your computer is drive A. If you put the disk in there, type **a:** and press **Enter**. Drive B is the lower disk drive, or the one on the right. If you put the disk in it, type **b:** and press **Enter**.
3. When you see the A:\> or B:\> prompt, type **install** and press **Enter**.
4. Follow the instructions on your screen. Most people find that the Basic installation program is the right one to use.

Choosing Programs to Install

If you install everything, WordPerfect 5.1 takes up about 4 Mb of space on your hard disk. To save disk space, you may choose not to install some of the program's features, if you're certain you won't be using them. Just be sure to install the rest! Here are some guidelines to help you respond to the prompts that appear on the screen asking which parts of the program you want to install.

UTILITY PROGRAMS

It's highly recommended that you install the Utility Files. These include the installation program itself, which enables you to install updated versions of Word-Perfect later.

TUTORIALS

If you're not planning to take the tutorial lessons, you may choose not to install the Learning files. Think about this carefully, though, because the tutorial lessons, which you work through along with the *Word-Perfect Workbook* that comes with the program, are excellent for beginners.

HELP

Be sure to install the Help files. This built-in utility is really valuable in a feature-rich program such as Word-Perfect. It can save you many trips to the manual as you're learning the program's basics, and even after you begin to use its more sophisticated features.

KEYBOARD FILES

If you're not planning to do specialized typing, such as equations, don't install the keyboard files.

STYLE LIBRARY

The Style Library contains predefined formats, called Styles. Most people find that these styles save time when creating documents that incorporate several different formats. It's not a bad idea to install this feature.

WORDPERFECT

Obviously, you want to install the WordPerfect Program! Be sure to say Yes at this prompt.

SPELLER/THESAURUS

Install the Speller, too. It's invaluable for correcting your typing mistakes. You can skip the Thesaurus if you don't think you'll use it very often to find alternates for words.

PRINTER

You can probably skip the Printer program. Most people never use this one, because you can print documents without it. It's a highly technical utility that lets you modify your printer.

GRAPHICS

If you want to use the graphic images that come with WordPerfect, be sure to install these files.

After WordPerfect has installed its files, it checks two special files that are read each time you start your computer. The file named CONFIG.SYS has to allow twenty files to be open at the same time, so if the installation program finds that that this file needs to be changed, type **y** to let it make the change. The installation program also checks the AUTOEXEC.BAT file on your computer to see that the proper command is inserted there, which enables you to run WordPerfect from any directory in your computer's filing system. So yes, let it do this.

Installing Printers

Next, you install your printer. Just follow the on-screen instructions. And be sure to install *all* the printers for which you plan to format documents, not just the printer that's connected to your computer. If you have a different printer at work, for example, install it, too, so you can format documents for that printer when you work at home. If you're installing WordPerfect on a laptop, install the printers that you'll probably have access to on your trip. Installing an HP LaserJet is a good bet, for example, as that model is widely used.

When the installation is done, remove the floppy disk from the drive. Then, if you let the installation program change your AUTOEXEC.BAT or CONFIG.SYS files, press **Ctrl-Alt-Del** to restart your computer.

Now you're ready to start the program.

3

Starting and Exiting WordPerfect

Once WordPerfect is installed on your computer, all you have to do to start the program is type **wp** when you see the DOS prompt.

You can type **wp** and start WordPerfect from any directory on your computer *if* you let the installation program change your AUTO-EXEC.BAT file in the previous lesson. If you didn't, however, you'll have to change to the directory that WordPerfect is in each time you want to run the program. It's usually in C:\WP51, so you'll have to type **cd \wp51** and press **Enter**, and *then*, at the prompt, type **wp** and press **Enter** to start WordPerfect.

The WordPerfect Screen

When WordPerfect starts, you won't see much. The program presents a clean screen, much like a blank sheet of typing paper. A short, horizontal blinking line,

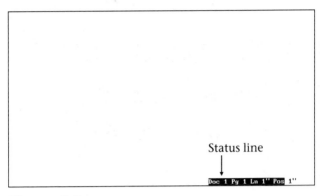

Status line

Figure 3.1   WordPerfect's editing screen

called a *cursor*, appears in the upper left-hand corner of the screen. As you type, the characters appear just to the left of the cursor. In the lower right-hand corner of the screen is a *status line* that shows which document you're in (1 or 2), which page you're on, and the position of the cursor (Figure 3.1).

▷ **Note:** If someone else has set up WordPerfect for you, you may see centimeters (c), points (p), or "WordPerfect units" (w) instead of inches (") on the status line. These are alternate units of measure.

The Keyboard

Before you start typing on that clean sheet of "paper," though, take some time to get acquainted with a few of the specialized keys on your keyboard (Figure 3.2). (We discuss using a mouse, which is an alternate way of using WordPerfect, in Chapter 6.)

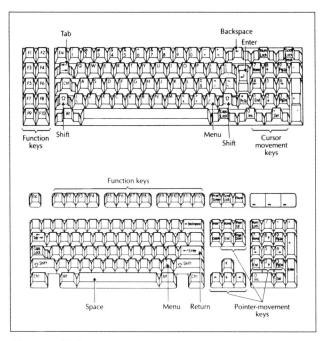

Figure 3.2 A computer keyboard, with function keys (a) at the side and across the top (b)

The Function Keys

Depending on which type of keyboard you're using, the function keys may be on the left side of the keyboard or across the top. Some keyboards have them in both places.

In WordPerfect, one way to give commands to the program is to use these function keys. Each key can give four commands—one when you press it by itself, another when you press it with the Ctrl key, a third when you press it with the Shift key, and the fourth when you press it with the Alt key. For example:

- Pressing **F3** by itself gets you Help.
- Pressing **Shift-F3** switches you from Document 1 to Document 2, and back again if you press it a second time.
- Pressing **Alt-F3** shows you the normally invisible codes that format your document behind the scenes. (If you try this now, you'll just see a split screen unless you've typed and formatted some text. Press **Alt-F3** again to return to the regular screen.)
- Pressing **Ctrl-F3** brings up a menu with three other commands on it.

You'll learn what the rest of the function keys do later in the book.

The Character Keys

The vast majority of the keys on your keyboard are easy to recognize—they're the letter and number keys, just like on a typewriter. A few of the other keys also work just like a typewriter:

- **Shift**—Press to uppercase a single character.
- **Caps Lock**—Press it, and all letters you type will appear in ALL CAPS.
- **Tab**—May be labeled "Tab" and has two arrows on it, pointing in opposite directions. It indents text one tab space, usually five characters.

The Special Keys

Some of the keys, however, have uses specific only to a computer and WordPerfect. They are:

Backspace   Located at the upper right-hand corner of the character keys, just above the Enter key. Press it to erase the character(s) to the left of the cursor.

Del or **Delete**   Press it to erase the character(s) to the right of the cursor. (There may be more than one Del key on your keyboard—one on the numeric keypad and another above the arrow keys.)

Ins or **Insert**   Press it to change the way characters are inserted as you type. If you press Ins, the message "Typeover" appears in the bottom left of the screen, which means any characters you type appear *over* characters to the right of them on the screen (thereby deleting them).

Tip

Typeover isn't a very efficient way of correcting mistakes. It's best to leave the program in Insert mode so that characters aren't replaced by what you type. Use the Backspace and Delete keys to delete characters you don't want.

Esc or **Escape**   Press it twice to cancel a command or to back out of a menu without making any choices. (You'll see how to use menus in Lesson 6.)

The Esc key has a different use in WordPerfect than in other computer programs, in which Esc works as a Cancel key. In WordPerfect, the F1 function key is the Cancel key. Use the Esc key in WordPerfect to repeat a character a specified number of times. For example, if you press Esc, you'll see a message, "Repeat Value = 8," at the lower right of your screen. If you type a character while that message is showing, it will repeat eight times.

Any character key that you press and hold down will repeat. This is called *typematic* on a computer. Try it and see.

The Numeric Keypad

The numeric keypad, on the right of most keyboards, is designed to let you enter numbers and data quickly. In WordPerfect, however, you won't be entering huge amounts of data—it's not a spreadsheet program—so the numeric keypad serves a special purpose: it lets you move through your document. You control how this works by using the Num Lock key at the top of the numeric keypad.

When the Num Lock light is on, the numeric keypad works like a calculator keypad, and you can use it for entering numbers. When the Num Lock light is off, you can use the keys to move through your documents, as you'll see in Lesson 5.

⇨ **Note:** Whenever you see the Pos indicator blinking on the screen, the Num Lock key is on. Normally, in WordPerfect, you don't want Num Lock on unless you're entering large amounts of numbers. Just press Num Lock to turn it off. Also note that when Num Lock is on, you won't be able to use the Delete key on the numeric keypad.

The Arrow Keys

To the left of the numeric keypad on many keyboards is a set of arrow keys, and keys marked "Home," "Page Up," "Page Down," and "End." As you might guess, these keys are used to move through your documents, and you'll see more about them in Lesson 5. If you don't have a set of these arrow keys, you can use the numeric keypad instead.

Exiting WordPerfect

Now that you've had a quick overview of how the keys work, let's exit from WordPerfect.

1. Press the **F7** key. That's the Exit key.
2. When the message, "Save document? Yes (No)" appears, type **n**.
3. Next, you'll see the message, "Exit WordPerfect? No (Yes)." Type **y**.

Tip
Whenever you have a Yes/No choice like this, WordPerfect shows you the most often used choice—or the safest choice—first. The alternate choice is in parentheses. Simply press Enter to accept the first choice, or type the letter of the choice you want.

Now that you know how to start WordPerfect and exit from it, you're ready to create a simple document in the next lesson.

4

Creating a Document

Now you're ready to put WordPerfect to work. You can start by typing the sample letter shown in Figure 4.1.

Starting WordPerfect Again

First, you'll need to start WordPerfect again, because you exited from it in Lesson 3.

At the DOS prompt (C\:> or D\:>) type **wp** and then press **Enter**.

You'll see the blank editing screen. The cursor will be at the very top, on Ln 1 Pos 1". It's at the 1-inch position because WordPerfect is preset to have one-inch margins on the right, left, top, and bottom.

If you have a mouse, you'll also see a larger rectangular cursor. As you move the mouse on your desktop, that cursor moves on the screen. Remember, you'll learn to use the mouse in Lesson 6.

```
Mr. Benjamin Jefferson
2100 Water St.
San Francisco, CA 94109

Dear Ben,

It was great to hear from you last week and catch up on all the
family news. Congradtulations on Martha's graduation, by the way.

We're planning a family campiong trip to Yosemite next week and
wondering if you and your family would like to meet us there. I
hear the fishing is excellent at at this time of the year.

We'll be camping at Frenchman's Meadow from Thursady, August 26
to Sunday, August 29. If you think you'd like to go, give me a
call at work as soon as you can. The number is (415) 555-1234.


Best,


Your Name
```
`Doc 1 Pg 1 Ln 1" Pos 1"`

Figure 4.1   The sample letter

General Guidelines

If you haven't typed with a word processing program before, you may not be aware that it works a little bit differently from a typewriter. As you type, keep in mind the following:

1. *Don't* press Enter at the end of a line. Just keep on typing and watch how the words wrap to the next line. Press Enter *only* when you want to end one paragraph and begin another. If you want to insert a blank line, press Enter twice.
2. Don't press the Spacebar twice after periods. (This is a hard habit to break.) The typefaces your computer uses adjust for the spaces between sentences. Really.
3. Don't worry about making mistakes as you type. You can use the Speller to correct your document later, as you'll see.

The Letter

The Address

To type the recipient's address, follow these steps:

1. Type **Mr. Benjamin Jefferson** and press **Enter**.
2. Type **2100 Water St.** and press **Enter**.
3. Type **San Francisco, CA 94109** and press **Enter**.
4. Press **Enter** twice to create a blank line.
5. Type **Dear Ben,** and press **Enter** twice for another blank line.

The Body of the Letter

Now you're ready to start typing the paragraphs in the letter. Remember to follow the guidelines above and just keep on typing each paragraph as though it were just one long line. The program will break the lines as you reach the right-hand margin.

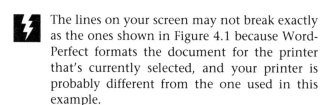 The lines on your screen may not break exactly as the ones shown in Figure 4.1 because Word-Perfect formats the document for the printer that's currently selected, and your printer is probably different from the one used in this example.

1. Type the first paragraph, *including* the mistakes: **It was great to hear from you last week and catch up on all the family news. Con-**

gradtulations on Martha's graduation, by the way.

2. Press **Enter** twice at the end of the paragraph, once to end the paragraph and another time to insert a blank line.

3. Type the second paragraph, including errors: **We're planning a family campoing trip to Yosemite next week and wondering if you and your family would like to meet us there. I hear the fishing is excellent at at this time of the year.**

4. Press **Enter** twice at the end of the paragraph, once to end the paragraph and another time to insert a blank line.

5. Type the next paragraph, again including errors: **We'll be camping at Frenchman's Meadow from Thursady, August 26 to Sunday, August 29. If you think you'd like to go, give me a call at work as soon as you can. The number is (415) 555-1234.**

6. Press **Enter** three times this time to insert two blank lines.

7. Type the closing: Press **Tab** to indent the line. Then type **Best,** and press **Enter** three times to leave room for your signature.

⇨ **Note:** WordPerfect is preset with a tab every half inch. To align text neatly, one line above another, don't press the Spacebar to insert spaces. Always use the Tab key instead. (The Tab can be reset to a different value.)

8. Press **Tab** and type **Your Name** (substitute your name here).

We've included a couple of mistakes for the Speller to catch. If you make additional mistakes and want to correct them now, just press the Right or Left arrow keys to move to the right of the character, press the Backspace key to erase your mistake, and then type the correct character.

Congratulations! You've just created a letter in WordPerfect. You'll learn different ways later to correct the errors you deliberately inserted.

Saving the Letter

If you were to exit WordPerfect now, without saving the letter, you wouldn't be able to get it back later; you'd have to retype the whole thing. In general, it's a good idea to save every document you create so you can revise it at a later date, if you want to. And, if you've just written a short note, you may not be ready to print it as soon as you finish it. If you save it, you can print it later, along with a few other documents that you're planning to print. This also prevents switching your printer on and off repeatedly.

1. To save the letter, press the Save key, **F10**.
2. To name this letter MYLETTER, type **myletter** at the "Document to be saved:" prompt in the lower left-hand corner of the screen.
3. When your document is saved, you'll see C:\WP51\MYLETTER on the status line (Figure 4.2). This tells you that the document is saved in the directory named WP51 on drive C, which was automatically created for you when you installed WordPerfect. If WordPerfect is stored on a different drive or in a different directory on your com-

puter, the status line will read differently.(You'll learn more about saving and naming documents in Lesson 9.)

There's another way to save a document if you're through using WordPerfect and want to exit from the program at the same time. But before we show you that trick, we're going to add some text to this document in the next lesson, so don't exit from WordPerfect now.

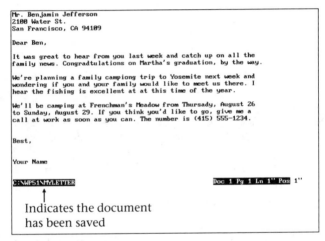

```
Mr. Benjamin Jefferson
2100 Water St.
San Francisco, CA 94109

Dear Ben,

It was great to hear from you last week and catch up on all the
family news. Congradtulations on Martha's graduation, by the way.

We're planning a family campiong trip to Yosemite next week and
wondering if you and your family would like to meet us there. I
hear the fishing is excellent at at this time of the year.

We'll be camping at Frenchman's Meadow from Thursady, August 26
to Sunday, August 29. If you think you'd like to go, give me a
call at work as soon as you can. The number is (415) 555-1234.


Best,


Your Name


C:\WP51\MYLETTER                                    Doc 1 Pg 1 Ln 1" Pos 1"
```

Indicates the document
has been saved

Figure 4.2   The saved document

5

Working with Longer Documents

The letter you just typed fills only one screen. Normally, most of the documents you write probably will be a little longer than this letter. So, to give you some practice in moving around in a longer document, you can add some text to your original letter.

Adding a New Paragraph

If you haven't moved it from the previous lesson, the cursor should be at the end of the document, just after your name.

Tip

If the cursor isn't at the end of the document, there's a quick way to put it there: press Home twice; then press End.

1. Press the **Up arrow** key 9 times to move the cursor to the line just before the last paragraph

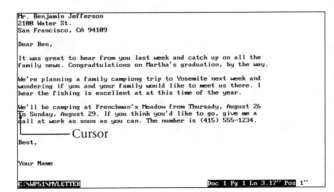

```
Mr. Benjamin Jefferson
2100 Water St.
San Francisco, CA 94109

Dear Ben,

It was great to hear from you last week and catch up on all the
family news. Congradtulations on Martha's graduation, by the way.

We're planning a family campiong trip to Yosemite next week and
wondering if you and your family would like to meet us there. I
hear the fishing is excellent at at this time of the year.

We'll be camping at Frenchman's Meadow from Thursady, August 26
To Sunday, August 29. If you think you'd like to go, give me a
call at work as soon as you can. The number is (415) 555-1234.
                ———— Cursor
Best,

Your Name
```
`C:\WP51\MYLETTER`   `Doc 1 Pg 1 Ln 3.17" Pos 1"`

Figure 5.1   Moving the cursor

(starting with "We'll be camping") as shown in
Figure 5.1. (You can use the arrow keys to move
the cursor up, down, left, and right.)

2. Press **Enter** to insert a blank line.
3. Now type a new paragraph: **We already have a
   big assortment of poles and equipment, so
   all you'll need to bring is a tent and your
   appetites.** Press **Enter** for another blank line.
   See Figure 5.2.

Navigating a Document

There are all sorts of ways to move through a document in WordPerfect. You've already seen that you can
move the cursor character by character with the Right
and Left arrow keys, and up and down lines by pressing
the Up and Down arrow keys. Try out some of these
techniques with the document on the screen.

```
It was great to hear from you last week and catch up on all the
family news. Congradtulations on Martha's graduation, by the way.

We're planning a family campiong trip to Yosemite next week and
wondering if you and your family would like to meet us there. I
hear the fishing is excellent at at this time of the year.

We already have a big assortment of poles and equipment, so all
you'll need to bring is a tent and your appetites.

We'll be camping at Frenchman's Meadow from Thursady, August 26
to Sunday, August 29. If you think you'd like to go, give me a
call at work as soon as you can. The number is (415) 555-1234.

Best,


Your Name


C:\WP51\MYLETTER                         Doc 1 Pg 1 Ln 3.33" Pos 6"
```

Figure 5.2   Inserting a new paragraph

1. To move to the beginning of the document, press **Home** twice, then press the **Up arrow** key.
2. To move to the end of the current line, press **Home** once, then press the **Right arrow** key.
3. To move to the beginning of the line, press **Home** once, then press the **Left arrow** key.

Tip

To return to the previous cursor position, press Ctrl-Home twice. Remember this tip! It can save you lots of time in figuring out where you were, and then moving back there.

You can also move screen by screen.

1. To move to the top of the screen, press the **Minus** (–) key on the numeric keypad.
2. To move to the bottom of the screen, press the **Plus** (+) key on the numeric keypad.

You can't move the cursor beyond the end of what you've typed unless you insert blank lines at the end of a document (by pressing Enter); then you can move the cursor through the blank lines.

These are just a few of the ways you can move through a document. Table 5.1 summarizes these and shows you some others.

Table 5.1 Moving through a Document

Press This Key Combination	To Move the Cursor
Right and Left arrow keys	Character by character
Up and Down arrow keys	Line by line
Ctrl-Right arrow or Ctrl-Left arrow	Word by word
Home-Right arrow or Home-Left arrow	To the end or beginning of a line
Home-Up arrow or Home-Down arrow	To the top or bottom of the screen
PgDn or PgUp	To the next or previous page
Ctrl-Home *<page number>* Enter	To the page number you enter
Home Home Up arrow or Home Home Down arrow	To the end or beginning of the document

Tip

Use the arrow keys for short-distance moving only. And the mouse is probably faster to use than the arrow keys for short-distance moves. If you want to move the cursor to a place you can see on the screen, just move the mouse pointer there and click the left mouse button. The other key combinations are more efficient for moving long distances—to places you can't see on the screen.

When you feel comfortable with these techniques for moving through documents, it's time to go on to the next lesson. You don't have to memorize all these key combinations now. Refer to this table later when you need to refresh your memory.

Saving and Exiting

You've made some changes to this document, and you'll want to save it because you're going to use it again. (Remember, always save any document that you want to keep.)

This time, however, you'll save the document and exit WordPerfect at the same time. Instead of using the F10 (Save) key, use the F7 (Exit) key.

1. Press **F7**.
2. When you see the "Save Document: Yes (No)" prompt, type **y**.
3. When the "Document to be saved:" prompt appears with the name you gave the document,

MYLETTER, at the end, type **y** to save the document again, using the same name.

Tip
You could enter a different name for the document if you wanted to save both versions of it.
The original letter would remain unchanged,
and this new version would be saved under the
new name, such as MYLET2.

4. You'll see the message "Exit WP? No (Yes)". Type
   y to exit WordPerfect. If you typed n for No at
   this prompt, you'd stay in WordPerfect.

6

Working with WordPerfect Menus

Until now, you've used the keyboard and the function keys to tell WordPerfect what you want it to do. There's another way to give commands to the program, and that's by using menus, with or without a mouse. Menus are easier to use than memorizing the function key commands, because you can see the choices right there on the screen.

Start WordPerfect again to follow along in this lesson. At the "C:\> or D:\>" prompt, type **wp** and then press **Enter**.

Using a Mouse

As you learned in the previous lesson, you can use a mouse with WordPerfect 5.1. During installation, simply tell the program what kind of mouse you have. If you use a mouse, you'll find that operations like selecting large blocks of text and moving the cursor are somewhat easier than using just the keyboard. But using a mouse is completely optional.

The rectangular cursor on the screen is the *mouse pointer.* As you move the mouse, the pointer moves on the editing screen. In fact, you probably won't see the mouse pointer at all until you start to move the mouse.

There are three basic techniques to master when using the mouse: clicking, double-clicking, and dragging.

To click on a menu item to select it, move the mouse pointer on it and click the left mouse button. This is the technique you'll use most often in WordPerfect.

To double-click on an item, press the left mouse button twice, quickly. You won't need to double-click in WordPerfect 5.1 for DOS, but you will in Word-Perfect for Windows.

To drag, press the left mouse button, keep it down, and move the mouse. Dragging is a fast way to select large amounts of text.

As you learn to use the menu system, you'll see that you can use it with the keyboard, with the mouse, or with a combination of both.

Opening the Main Menu

To activate WordPerfect's menu system, press **Alt-=**. (Hold down the Alt key and type =.) If you have a mouse, just press the right mouse button to display the menu.

Tip
You can set up WordPerfect so all you have to do is press the Alt key to pull down menus. To do this, press Shift-F1 (Setup). Then type d for Display and m for Menu Options. Type a for Alt Key Selects Pull-Down Menus and y for Yes.

Then press F7 to return to your document. It's a good idea to do this so that the menus will be easier to use.

Opening Other Menus

Once you see the Main menu bar (Figure 6.1), you can press the Right and Left arrow keys to move through the choices that are listed. To open one of those menus, press **Enter** or the **Down arrow** key, or click on a choice with the mouse.

Let's see how this works.

1. Press **Alt** (or **Alt-=**, if you didn't adjust Word-Perfect to use the Alt key, as explained in the Tip above).
2. Press the **Right arrow** key to highlight the Edit menu. Then press **Enter**. You'll see the same Edit menu as in Figure 6.2.

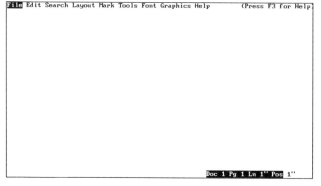

Figure 6.1 The Main menu bar

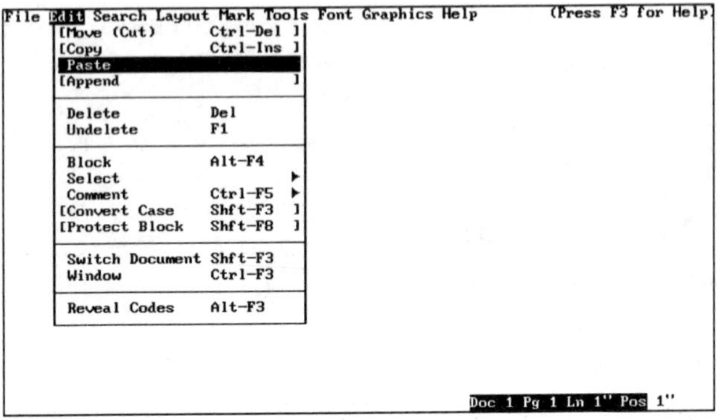

```
File Edit Search Layout Mark Tools Font Graphics Help        (Press F3 for Help)
     [Move (Cut)    Ctrl-Del ]
     [Copy          Ctrl-Ins ]
      Paste
     [Append                 ]

      Delete        Del
      Undelete      F1

      Block         Alt-F4
      Select                  ▶
      Comment       Ctrl-F5   ▶
     [Convert Case  Shft-F3  ]
     [Protect Block Shft-F8  ]

      Switch Document Shft-F3
      Window        Ctrl-F3

      Reveal Codes  Alt-F3

                                         Doc 1 Pg 1 Ln 1'' Pos 1''
```

Figure 6.2   The Edit menu

USING HOT KEYS

You also can just type **e** to choose the Edit menu. All of the menus can be opened by using what are called *hot keys*, the first letter of their names—except the Font menu. Because File also starts with an F, the Font menu is accessed by typing **o**. So, pressing Alt-E opens the Edit menu, Alt-F opens the File menu, and so forth. Once a menu is displayed, you can type the high-lighted letter of any item to select it.

MENU SIGNALS

An *arrowhead* next to a menu choice means that if you choose that item, you'll see another menu. For example, in Figure 6.2, if you choose Select, you'll see another menu.

Brackets around an item means that it can't be selected currently. Notice that the Copy command in Figure 6.2 is in brackets; obviously, you can't copy something unless you've selected some text first. After you've selected some text, the Copy command will be available.

Keyboard shortcuts are the key combinations listed next to menu commands. They indicate the letters to type to access a particular command instead of opening the menu to do so. In Figure 6.2 you can see that Del is a shortcut for Delete, and F1 is a shortcut for Undelete.

Canceling a Menu Selection

If you change your mind about using a menu, there's an easy way to back out of the menu without making any selection at all. Just press **Esc** or **F1**, the Cancel key. That will take you back, one menu at a time.

 Tip
To back out of the whole menu system at once so that the Main menu isn't displayed at the top of the screen, press F7 (Exit). If you have a mouse, clicking the right mouse button will do the same thing.

Pull-Down Menu Practice

To get some experience in all the different ways of using the pull-down menu system, take these steps:

1. Open the Main menu bar, if it isn't already displayed. Press **Alt** (or **Alt-=**).
2. Type **t** to view the Tools menu.
3. Press **Esc** to return to the Main menu without making a choice.

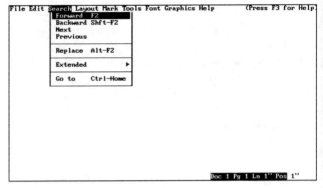

Figure 6.3 The Search menu

4. Use the **Left arrow** key to move to the Search menu. Then press **Enter** to open it (Figure 6.3).
5. Press the **Down arrow** key until you highlight **Extended**. Another menu will appear (Figure 6.4).
6. Press **F1** twice to return to the Main menu.
7. If you are using a mouse, click with the left mouse button on the Help menu. Click on Index to see the Help index, or drag the mouse pointer down to Index and then release the mouse button. Click with the right mouse button to return to the editing screen.

Don't worry about all the things you see on these menus now; the important thing in this lesson is to learn how to navigate them.

You can use any combination of these techniques— typing the highlighted letter of a menu name, moving to an item with the arrow keys and pressing Enter, or clicking with the mouse—to make selections from

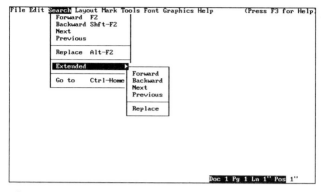

Figure 6.4   The Extended Search menu

menus. For example, you might press Alt and type F to open the File menu. Then you might click with the mouse on the Print command to choose it. Or you could press Shift-F7 to go directly to the full-screen Print menu.

Tip
Many people find that using the highlighted mnemonic letters is the easiest way to use WordPerfect menus. For example, all you have to do to save a document is press Alt, type f for File, and then type s for Save.

Using Bottom Menus

There's another type of menu in WordPerfect—bottom menus. Also called status line menus, they appear at the bottom of the screen any time you need to be able

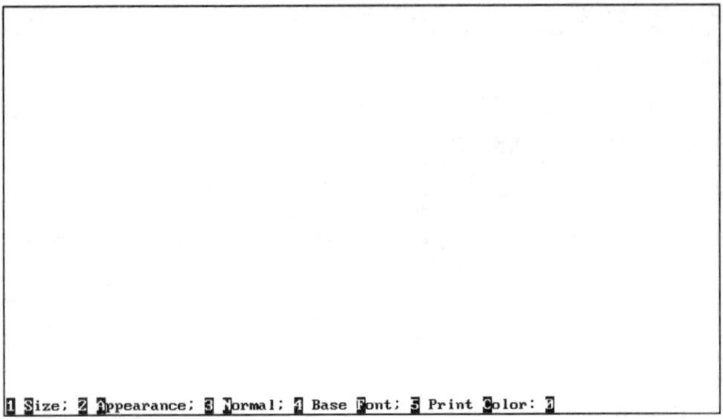

```
─────────────────────────────────────────────
│                                             │
│                                             │
│                                             │
│                                             │
│                                             │
│                                             │
│                                             │
│                                             │
│                                             │
│                                             │
│ 1 Size; 2 Appearance; 3 Normal; 4 Base Font; 5 Print Color: 3 │
─────────────────────────────────────────────
```

Figure 6.5 The Font menu on the status line

to see the text on the screen, which the pull-down menus may hide.

To see how these menus work, press **Ctrl-F8** to bring up the Font menu across the bottom of the screen. With the menu in that location, you can see text at the same time (Figure 6.5).

Selecting from Bottom Menus

To access the choices from bottom menus, you can type the highlighted letter or number or click on them with the left mouse button. (We'll only be using the highlighted letters in this book, not numbers.) Note that the arrow keys don't work in bottom menus.

Canceling a Bottom Menu

To cancel a bottom menu without making any choices from it, use the Esc key, the F1 key, or the F7 key. You can also choose option 0 or click with the right mouse button.

Using Full-Screen Menus

A third type of menu appears in WordPerfect when there are just too many things to choose from, and they all won't fit onto a pull-down menu or display across the screen in a bottom menu. Look at the Print menu (Figure 6.6) as an example of working with a full-screen menu.

Selecting from Full-Screen Menus

You can't use the arrow keys to make choices from a full-screen menu, but you can use the keyboard (just type the highlighted letter or number of your choice) or the mouse (just click on the item you want to choose).

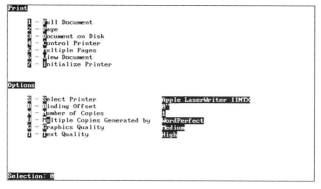

Figure 6.6 The Print menu

Canceling a Full-Screen Menu

To cancel a full-screen menu without making any choices is the same as canceling a bottom menu: use the Esc key, the F1 key, or the F7 key. You can also choose option 0 or click with the right mouse button.

Combining Menu Techniques

At this point, you've been exposed to a number of different techniques for making choices from menus in WordPerfect. If everything seems a bit overwhelming at first, be patient, and remember, you can use any combination of these techniques with the program. Stick to methods you're comfortable with until you get used to the way WordPerfect works; then experiment a little to increase your flexibility.

Use the Menus

Because using menus is so much easier than using the function keys, we recommend that you use them initially. In fact, you'll be using menus for the lessons in this book. Later, when you want more speed from the program, you'll find that using the function keys is faster than using the menus. But until you get accustomed to WordPerfect, using the menu system is the best way. You'll take a closer look at the function keys in the next chapter, however, so that when you're ready to use this method, you'll have the information at hand.

7

Working with Function Keys

Function Key Templates

You received two function key templates with the program—one to place over the function keys on the side and another that rests across the top of the keyboard. If you didn't put them on your keyboard already, do so now. They'll be a big help as you get used to the program.

Tip

If you've misplaced your function key template, there's an easy way to determine what the keys do and replace the template at the same time. Press F3 twice to access an on-screen display of the template (Figure 7.1). If your keyboard has function keys on the side, type 1 to see that arrangement (Figure 7.2). With your printer turned on, press the Print Screen key to print a copy of the function key template that's being displayed. Once you have a printed copy, you can post it near your computer and refer to it whenever you need it.

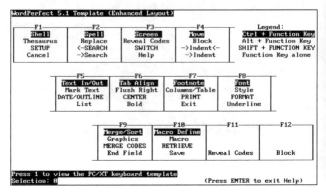

Figure 7.1   One of the function key templates

Don't worry, you don't have to memorize all the key combinations—that's what the template is for. In fact, you'll probably never use most of them. In this book we concentrate on the keys you'll use most often.

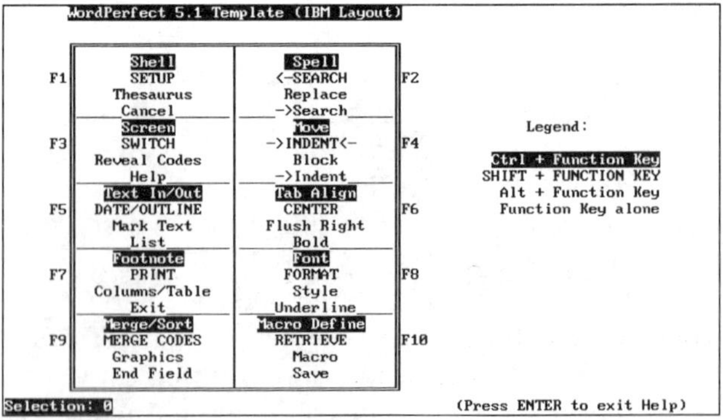

Figure 7.2   The other function key template

Color Coding

With WordPerfect, you also were given a sheet of colored decals to put on your Ctrl, Shift, and Alt keys. These decals can help you see at a glance which keys to press as you look at the color-coded template that came with the program.

Red = Ctrl key
Green = Shift key
Blue = Alt key
Black = function key by itself (There's no decal for this one.)

Why Use the Function Keys?

As mentioned, it's best to use the menus as you're getting used to the program. You can easily see which commands are listed on the menus before you make your choice. As you look at the menus, you'll also get an idea of the features WordPerfect contains. But using the function keys is faster and requires fewer keystrokes, so it's popular with touch typists who know the program pretty well. For example, to save a document using the menu system, you have to press Alt (or Alt-=), F, and S, but using the function keys you only have to press F10.

The Most Popular Function Keys

There are relatively a few function key combinations that most people use daily. Most of the others are for fairly advanced features that aren't used as frequently, such as graphics, footnotes, and equations. Here are the ten most often used, "everyday" function key combinations that you will see mentioned in various places throughout this book:

F10	Save—saves the document you're working on.
Shift-F10	Retrieve—retrieves a document you've created.
Shift-F7	Exit—saves and exits WordPerfect.
F1	Cancel or Undelete—cancels a menu choice or undoes a deletion.
F3	Help—gives information about what you're doing.
F2	Spell—runs the spell checker.
F5	List Files—displays a list of the documents you've created.
Shift-F3	Switch—goes from one document to another.
Ctrl-F8	Font—switches to a different typeface.
Shift-F8	Format—changes margins, line spacing, and so forth.

As you become accustomed to WordPerfect, you may want to memorize these ten function key combinations after you're comfortable with the menu system.

8

Getting Help

WordPerfect has a built-in Help system that explains every feature of the program and how to use it. You can spend hours exploring this fascinating feature if you want to learn more about how the program works and what it can do. Using Help is much faster than reading the manual, too.

Help—The F3 Key

At any time while you're using WordPerfect, Help is just one keystroke away, and that key is F3. (In many other word processing programs, the Help key is F1.) Pressing this key brings up the program's first Help screen (Figure 8.1).

You can, of course, also use the menu system to access Help. Press **Alt** and type **h** for the Help menu. If you want to see the list of Help topics, press **Alt** and type **h** and then **i** (for Index).

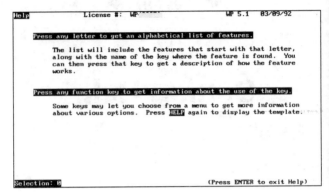

Figure 8.1 The Help instruction screen

The First Help Screen

The first Help screen gives you instructions for getting help, but it also provides some other useful information. At the top of the screen is your license number, if you typed it in during the installation process. At the upper right-hand corner of the screen is the date of your WordPerfect release. WordPerfect Corporation issues interim releases from time to time, and if you call for technical support, you may get asked about which release you have. Look at the Help screen to find out!

As you can see from this screen, you can type any letter to see an alphabetical list of the features that begin with that letter. Let's see how this works.

1. To get help on centering text, for example, type **c**. The screen changes to show you the topics beginning with C (Figure 8.2). If the topic you're looking for isn't listed there, type that letter again to see more topics. Notice that at the bottom of

```
Features [C]                        WordPerfect Key  Keystrokes

Cancel                              Cancel           F1
Cancel Hyphenation Code             Home             Home,/
Cancel Print Job(s)                 Print            Shft-F7,4,1
Capitalize Block (Block On)         Switch           Shft-F3,1
Cartridges and Fonts                Print            Shft-F7,s,3,4
Case Conversion (Block On)          Switch           Shft-F3
Center Block (Block On)             Center           Shft-F6
Center Justification                Format           Shft-F8,1,3,2
Center Page (Top to Bottom)         Format           Shft-F8,2,1
Center Tab Setting                  Format           Shft-F8,1,8,c
Center Text                         Center           Shft-F6
Centered Text With Dot Leaders      Center           Shft-F6,Shft-F6
Centimeters, Units of Measure       Setup            Shft-F1,3,8
Change Comment to Text              Text In/Out       Ctrl-F5,4,3
Change Default Directory            List             F5,=,Dir name,Enter
Change Font                         Font             Ctrl-F8
Change Supplementary Dictionary     Spell            Ctrl-F2,4
Change Text to Comment (Block On)  Text In/Out       Shft-F5
Character Sets                      Compose          Ctrl-v or Ctrl-2
Character Spacing                   Format           Shft-F8,4,6,3
More... Press c to continue.

Selection: 0                                (Press ENTER to exit Help)
```

Figure 8.2 Listing Help topics

Figure 8.2 it says "More... Press c to continue."
That indicates there are more topics beginning
with C.

2. To see the instructions for centering text, press
the keystrokes listed for that topic—in this case,
Shift-F6. You'll see the Help screen for centering
text (Figure 8.3).

➩ **Note:** The Help screens use the number equiv-
alents of the menu commands as well as the hot
key letters. Either way will work to carry out a
command. The numbers are remnants of earlier
versions of the WordPerfect program.

3. To exit from the Help system, either press **Enter**
or the **Spacebar**.

If you want to see a different list of alphabetical
topics, type another letter while you're in the Help
system. For example, to see topics on printing, type **p**.

```
Center
     Centers one or several lines between margins or over columns.  To place
     dot leaders in front of the centered text, press Center twice.  To create
     a Hard Center Tab on the next tab stop, press Home, Center.
   Between margins
     a.  To center a line, place the cursor at the left margin and press
         Center.  Any text typed will automatically be centered until Tab,
         Flush Right, or Enter is pressed.
     b.  With an existing line of text, press Center at the beginning of the
         line.  The line will be centered after you press Down Arrow or select
         an action that rewrites the screen.
   Over columns
     a.  Over a text column, press Center at the column's left margin.
     b.  Over a column created with tabs or indents, tab to where you want
         the text centered, press Center and type the text.
   Several lines
     You can center several lines by blocking the text and pressing Center.
     WordPerfect places a [Just:Center] code at the beginning of the block, and
     a [Just:] code at the end of the block.  The second justification code
     returns justification to its setting before the block.
   Selection: 0                                          (Press ENTER to exit Help)
```

Figure 8.3 Getting help on centering text

Tip

If your printer is turned on, you can print out the Help topic that's being displayed just by pressing the Print Screen key. Sometimes it's useful to have a paper copy to refer to when your computer's not on or so you don't have to interrupt on-screen work to summon the Help feature.

Help from Menus

If you have a menu pulled down, Help works a little differently. Pressing F3 with a menu displayed gets you *context-sensitive* help—help about what you're doing at that moment. Let's see how this works.

1. Press **Alt** and type **l** to open the Layout menu.
2. Press **F3** to get Help. You'll see a list of commands regarding the Layout menu (Figure 8.4).

```
Format: Line
    1 - Hyphenation
    2 - Hyphenation Zone
    3 - Justification
    4 - Line Height
    5 - Line Numbering
    6 - Line Spacing
    7 - Margins - Left and Right
    8 - Tab Set
    9 - Widow/Orphan Protection


Selection: 0                           (Press ENTER to exit Help)
```

Figure 8.4 Help on Layout menu commands

3. Type the highlighted number or letter of any topic to see its Help screen. For example, type **s** to see a Help screen on Line Spacing (Figure 8.5).

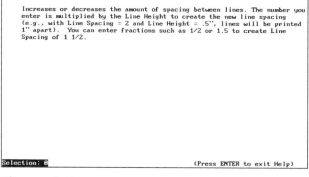

```
Line Spacing
    Increases or decreases the amount of spacing between lines. The number you
    enter is multiplied by the Line Height to create the new line spacing
    (e.g., with Line Spacing = 2 and Line Height = .5", lines will be printed
    1" apart). You can enter fractions such as 1/2 or 1.5 to create Line
    Spacing of 1 1/2.








Selection: 0                           (Press ENTER to exit Help)
```

Figure 8.5 Help on Line Spacing

You can't use the mouse in the Help system. You must type the highlighted letter or number to get the Help screen on that topic.

4. Press **Enter** or the **Spacebar** to exit Help and return to the Layout menu.

Helpful Hints

When you're in the Help system, you can press any function key combination to see what it does. This is a great way to get accustomed to the function key commands. To see the alphabetical topic list, type the letter of the feature you want instead of pressing a function key combination.

Some keys have their own Help screens: Esc, Tab and Shift-Tab, Backspace, the arrow keys (both the arrow keys on the numeric keyboard and the arrow keys on the main keyboard, if you have both sets), the hyphen key, Ins, Del, PgUp, PgDn, and the plus (+) and minus (–) keys on the numeric keypad. In addition, many Ctrl key combinations, such as Ctrl-Home (Go To), have their own Help screens.

◆ *Lesson* ◆

9

Saving a Document

As you have already learned, your work isn't saved until you tell WordPerfect to save it. Make it a habit to *save a document as soon as you've done some work that you don't want to lose.* In some cases, this could be after you've typed just one paragraph; in other cases, you might type a page or two before you want to save. And you'll definitely want to save the document you're working on before you exit WordPerfect, or you'll lose it all. Fortunately, the program will remind you to save before you exit.

There are two basic ways to save a document, which you saw in Lessons 4 and 5. Let's review them again quickly:

1. To save a document while you're in the process of creating it, press **F10** or choose **Save** from the File menu.
2. To save a document and then exit immediately from WordPerfect, press **F7** or choose **Exit** from the File menu.

Table 9.1 Rules for Naming Documents

Unacceptable Symbols	Acceptable Characters	Acceptable Sample Names
< > \	[ ] : , = + " ; /	Letters (either uppercase or lowercase)	LTTR MYLETTER MYLETTER.WPD SUE_LET.DOC
	Numbers (0–9)	SUSANS.LET MEMO1
	The symbols $ ~ # @ ! ' ( ) { } – _ ^ .	MEMO2.93 MEMO3.FEB MEMO#4

No matter which method you use, you'll be asked to give the document a name if you haven't saved it before.

Naming Documents

Your computer's operating system can read only eight-character file names, and it's pretty fussy about which characters you can and can't use (see Table 9.1). Therefore, you have to be fairly creative about giving names to documents that help you remember what they are. You can use fewer than eight characters if you want to, but anything over eight characters will just be deleted by the program.

In addition to the eight-character "first" name, you can add a period and a three-character extension ("last" name) to help you identify the type of document it is. For example, you might want to name a letter MYLETTER.WPD to identify this letter as created by WordPerfect (WPD standing for WordPerfect Document). You could also use a month or year abbreviation if you work with time-sensitive material, or use another extension that identifies the type of document, such as .LTR for letters and .RPT for reports. Some word processing programs automatically assign an extension to each document you create, but Word-Perfect doesn't.

"Save document?" Prompts

Depending on whether you're saving, or saving and exiting from WordPerfect, you'll get a different prompt. These prompts are designed to protect you from accidentally losing your work. They can be a little frustrating to understand, though.

Tip
To get out of the prompt loop without saving *or* exiting, press F1 for Cancel.

If you choose Save from the File menu or press F10, you'll get a "Document to be saved" prompt in the lower right-hand corner of the screen. If you haven't saved the document before, just type in a name and press Enter. It will automatically be stored in the directory WordPerfect is using for its document files, which is normally C:\WP51. All the files on your computer are stored in a system of directories, and each directory is separated from the one above it by a backslash. The letter that begins the name is the drive; the last name in the line is the name of the document.

If you've already saved the document at least once, you'll see its name. Press **Enter**, and you'll be asked whether you want to replace the existing version with the new version. If you want to replace the old version, type **y** for Yes. If you want to save the changed document under a different name, so that you have two versions of it, just press **End** to move the cursor to the end of the name the program is presenting, backspace over the old name, and type a new name.

The other names at the beginning of the prompt indicate the directory the document is stored in. Remember that WordPerfect normally stores documents in a directory named C:\WP51, so the prompt reads C:\WP51\MYLETTER, indicating that MYLETTER, which you saved earlier, is stored on drive C in a directory named WP51. If you want to store MYLETTER in a directory other than WP51, backspace over the WP51, enter a different directory name, and then enter the name you want the document to have. For example, to store MYLETTER in a directory named C:\DOCS, change the prompt to read C:\DOCS\MYLETTER, and then press **Enter**. Table 9.2 summarizes the methods for saving and exiting documents.

Tip
You can change the directory your files are automatically stored in by choosing Setup from the File menu and then selecting the Location of Files option.

Table 9.2 Saving and Exiting Methods

Action	Step 1	Step 2
Save your document and continue working on it.	Choose Save from the File menu or press F10.	Press Enter to accept the previous name or type a new name.
Save your document and close it.	Choose Exit from the File menu or press F7.	Answer Yes to the first prompt, No to the second.
Save your document and exit from WordPerfect.	Choose Exit from the File menu or press F7.	Answer Yes to both prompts.
Don't save the document, but stay in WordPerfect.	Choose Exit from the File menu or press F7.	Answer No to both prompts
Don't save the document, but exit from WordPerfect.	Choose Exit from the File menu or press F7.	Answer No to the first prompt, Yes to the second.

Automatic Saving

Some people make it a habit to give each new document a name as soon as they start typing it so they can use WordPerfect's built-in automatic saving feature.

Here's how it works. Once you've given a document a name, WordPerfect can automatically save your work for you every few minutes, so that if the power goes out you won't lose much. To turn on this neat feature:

1. Press **Shift-F1**, type **e** for Environment, and then type **b** for Backup Options.
2. You'll see the screen illustrated in Figure 9.1. Type **t** for Timed Backup; type **y** and enter the number of minutes you want to elapse between timed backups.
3. Press **Enter** and **F7** (Exit) to return to your screen.

Now, if the lights go out, you know that the program has automatically saved your work, at least up to the last few minutes. When you start the program again, you'll be able to retrieve the document, even though you couldn't save it yourself.

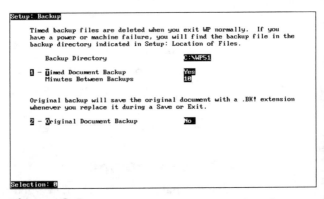

Figure 9.1 Turning on the Timed Backup feature

Always exit from WordPerfect before you turn your computer off. When you exit, you'll always get that "Save document?" prompt that will remind you to save your work.

You'll get some hands-on practice in saving documents in the next lesson.

◆ *Lesson* ◆

10

Opening and Closing a Document

Now that you've seen all the different ways you can save documents, let's try retrieving a document so you can get some practice.

Retrieving Your Letter

Remember the letter you created in Lesson 4? Open it now to use as a practice document. Start WordPerfect if it isn't already running. Then:

1. Choose **Retrieve** from the File menu or press **Shift-F10**.
2. At the "Document to be retrieved:" prompt, type **myletter** and press **Enter**.

Because MYLETTER is stored in WordPerfect's document directory, you don't have to enter any other directory name. The program automatically uses the C:\WP51 directory, or whichever directory you've specified with the Location of Files option.

Tip

You can start WordPerfect and open a document at the same time. At the DOS command line, enter the command used to start Word-Perfect, followed by the name of the document, and then press Enter. For example, to open MYLETTER when you start WordPerfect, type wp myletter at the C:\> prompt and press Enter.

If you want to retrieve a document in a different directory, you must enter that directory name before the document name, separated by backslashes. For example, to retrieve a document named YRLETTER in a directory named C:\WP51\SEPT, enter **c:\wp51\ sept\yrletter**. The document named MYLETTER should now be on your screen (Figure 10.1).

```
Benjamin Jefferson
2100 Water St.
San Francisco, CA 94109

Dear Ben,

It was great to hear from you last week and catch up on all the
family news. Congradtulations on Martha's graduation, by the way.

We're planning a family camping trip to Yosemite next week and
wondering if you and your family would like to meet us there. I
hear the fishing is excellent at at this time of the year.

We already have a big assortment of poles and equipment, so all
you'll need to bring is a tent and your appetites.

We'll be camping at Frenchman's Meadow from Thursady, August 26
to Sunday, August 29. If you think you'd like to go, give me a
call at work as soon as you can. The number is (415) 555-1234.

    Best,

C:\WP51\MYLETTER                              Doc 1 Pg 1 Ln 1" Pos 1"
```

Figure 10.1   Retrieving MYLETTER

Displaying Document Names with List Files

What if you don't remember the name of the document you want? Not to worry: WordPerfect has a List Files feature that shows you the names of the documents you've already created. When your memory fails you, it's handy to retrieve documents by using this feature. To see the List Files screen:

1. Choose **List Files** on the File menu, or press **F5**.
2. Press **Enter**. You'll see the files in your Word-Perfect directory (Figure 10.2). (Yours will look slightly different from these, depending on what's stored on your hard disk.)
3. Check to see that MYLETTER is really in that directory, by pressing the **Down arrow** key until MYLETTER comes into view. You'll see the date you saved MYLETTER and its size (in bytes).

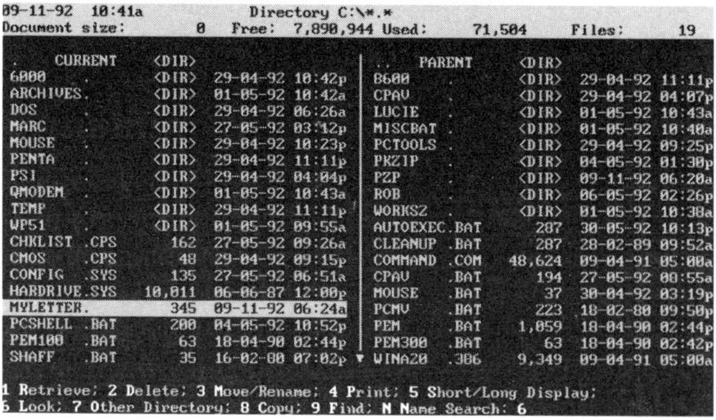

```
09-11-92  10:41a              Directory C:\*.*
Document size:       0    Free:  7,890,944 Used:     71,584    Files:       19

       CURRENT   <DIR>                         PARENT    <DIR>
6000           <DIR>  29-04-92 10:42p   8600           <DIR>  29-04-92 11:11p
ARCHIVES.      <DIR>  01-05-92 10:42a   CPAU           <DIR>  29-04-92 04:07p
DOS            <DIR>  29-04-92 06:26a   LUCIE          <DIR>  01-05-92 10:43a
MARC           <DIR>  27-05-92 03:12p   MISCBAT        <DIR>  01-05-92 10:40a
MOUSE          <DIR>  29-04-92 10:23p   PCTOOLS        <DIR>  29-04-92 09:25p
PENTA          <DIR>  29-04-92 11:11p   PKZIP          <DIR>  04-05-92 01:30p
PSI            <DIR>  29-04-92 04:04p   PZP            <DIR>  09-11-92 06:20a
QMODEM         <DIR>  01-05-92 10:43a   ROB            <DIR>  06-05-92 02:26p
TEMP           <DIR>  29-04-92 11:11p   WORKS2         <DIR>  01-05-92 10:38a
WP51           <DIR>  01-05-92 09:55a   AUTOEXEC.BAT      287  30-05-92 10:13p
CHKLIST  .CPS     162  27-05-92 09:26a   CLEANUP .BAT      287  28-02-89 09:52a
CMOS     .CPS      48  29-04-92 09:15p   COMMAND .COM   48,624  09-04-91 05:00a
CONFIG   .SYS     135  27-05-92 06:51a   CPAU    .BAT      194  27-05-92 00:55a
HARDRIVE.SYS   10,011  06-06-87 12:00p   MOUSE   .BAT       37  30-04-92 03:19p
MYLETTER.         345  09-11-92 06:24a   PCMU    .BAT      223  10-02-88 09:50p
PCSHELL .BAT      200  04-05-92 10:52p   PEM     .BAT    1,059  18-04-90 02:42p
PEM100  .BAT       63  18-04-90 02:44p   PEM300  .BAT       63  18-04-90 02:42p
SHAFF   .BAT       35  16-02-80 07:02p   WINA20  .386    9,349  09-04-91 05:00a

1 Retrieve; 2 Delete; 3 Move/Rename; 4 Print; 5 Short/Long Display;
6 Look; 7 Other Directory; 8 Copy; 9 Find; N Name Search: 6
```

Figure 10.2 The List Files screen

4. To retrieve a document from the List Files screen, highlight its name and then type **r** for Retrieve. But, since MYLETTER is already in the editing screen, press **F7** (Exit) to exit the List Files screen and return to your document.

Saving and Continuing to Work

At this point, make a few changes to MYLETTER—it doesn't matter what they are. Now, to understand how to save the letter with your changes and keep right on working on it:

1. Choose **Save** from the File menu or press **F10**.
2. At the prompt, press **Enter** and then type **y** for Yes to replace the former saved version of MYLETTER with the newer version you just made.

Saving and Clearing the Screen

Sometimes you'll want to close a document after you've saved it so you can open another one or create a new one. To save and close MYLETTER, thereby clearing the screen, take these steps:

1. Choose **Exit** from the File menu or press **F7**. (Don't worry; you're not going to exit!)
2. At the "Save document?" prompt, type **y**.
3. At the "Document to be saved:" prompt, press **Enter** to save the document under its current name.
4. At the "Replace C:\WP51\MYLETTER?" prompt, type **y** for Yes.
5. At the "Exit WP?" prompt, type **n** for No.

The screen will clear, and you'll stay in WordPerfect where you can keep on working.

 It's possible to retrieve a second document into a document you've already opened. All you need to do is choose Retrieve from the File menu again or press Shift-F10 and enter another document name. This feature is designed to let you combine smaller documents into one larger document, but it can also be frustrating if you're not aware of what's happening. If you don't want to combine documents, be sure to have a blank screen in front of you before you retrieve another document.

Now let's get MYLETTER back so you can practice with it some more. Choose **Retrieve** from the File menu (or press **Shift-F10**), type **myletter**, and press **Enter**.

Saving a Document onto a Floppy Disk

To save a document onto a floppy disk for safekeeping, or to work on it at a different computer, all you need to do is use the Save command and type the floppy drive letter (A or B) first, followed by a colon (:) and then the document name.

To try this, get out a formatted floppy disk and put it in drive A. (If you don't want to try it, skip to the next section, but keep MYLETTER on the screen.)

1. Choose **Save** from the File menu.
2. At the prompt, type **a:myletter**, press **Enter**.

The floppy drive will whir, and the status line will change to indicate that the version that's on the screen now is the one you just saved onto drive A. If you look in the lower left-hand corner of the screen, the status line now says A:\MYLETTER.

Clearing the Screen

Sometimes it's useful to be able to clear the screen without saving the document or exiting from Word-Perfect. This time, let's assume all you want to do is clear the screen without saving the document. Choose **Exit** from the File menu, but this time, type **n** for No in response to both prompts.

Your screen will clear, and you'll have a blank Document 1 editing screen, where you can start typing to create a new document, or choose Retrieve to open a document you've already created.

Opening the Document 2 Window

WordPerfect lets you open two documents at once. This feature is very useful if you want to be able to look into a different document and see what it says, or if you want to cut and paste blocks of text from one document into another, as you'll see in Lesson 17.

To open the second document window, all you need to do is choose **Switch Document** from the Edit menu, or press **Shift-F3**. Once you're in the Document 2 window, you can open another document. The status line will indicate which document window you're in (Figure 10.3).

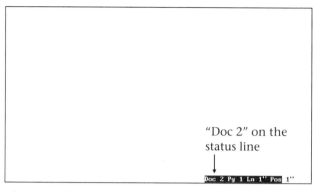

"Doc 2" on the
status line

↓

`Doc 2 Pg 1 Ln 1" Pos 1"`

Figure 10.3   Status line in a Document 2 window

Don't open *a second copy* of the *same document* or you may get hopelessly confused about which document has the most recent changes. If you do open a second copy of the same document, its name will be in brackets on the status line, like this: [C:\WP51\MYLETTER]. The brackets around the document name let you know you've got two copies of the same document open. If you try to save the one in brackets under the name that it already has, you'll get an "Access denied" message.

Exiting from WordPerfect

Had enough for now? Let's exit from WordPerfect and take a break.

1. Choose **Exit** from the File menu. Type **n** for No. You'll see the message "(Text was not modified)" to let you know that you haven't made any

changes since you last saved and it's OK to exit without saving. In this case, however, there wasn't any document on the screen, so the message did not appear.

2. At the "Exit WP?" prompt, type **y** for Yes.

If you had two documents open—one in the Document 1 window and the other in the Document 2 window—you'd be taken to the other document, where you could decide whether you wanted to save it, clear the screen without saving it, or exit from Word-Perfect.

You'll be amazed how quickly you'll get used to these saving and saving and exiting prompts. Before you know it, you'll automatically be pressing **F7 y Enter y** to save and exit, or **F10 Enter y** to save. It just seems tedious at first.

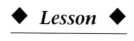

◆ *Lesson* ◆

11

Previewing a Document

Until now, the letter you've been working with has been viewed on the editing screen. But WordPerfect has a built-in feature called View Document that lets you see more exactly how your document is going to look when it's printed. It shows how it's positioned on the page, the font that's being used, page numbers (if you're using them), and so forth. If you don't like what you see, you can go back and change the document before you print it, which saves time and paper.

Previewing the Letter

To invoke this valuable feature, follow these steps:

1. Start WordPerfect and retrieve the sample **MYLETTER** or any other document you've already created.
2. Choose **Print** from the File menu or press **Shift-F7**. You'll see the Print menu.

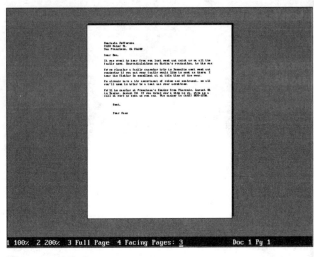

Figure 11.1   Previewing MYLETTER

3. Type **v** for View Document. Now you'll see
MYLETTER, or the document you retrieved, as
it will look when it's printed (Figure 11.1).

This is a graphical representation of the layout of the
letter. It's not exact, but it gives you a pretty good idea.

Zooming In

As you no doubt noticed, although View Document
gives you a good vantage point for layout, the type is
too small to read. WordPerfect solves that, too. You can
zoom in for a closer look at the page by choosing the
100% or 200% options; then scroll with the arrow keys.
If the document is longer than one page, you can also
choose to see facing pages (two pages placed side by
side), or press PgDn and PgUp to go from page to page.

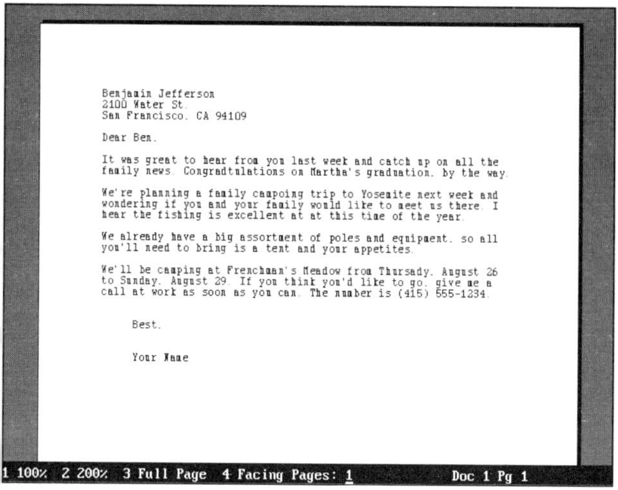

Figure 11.2 Looking at a 100% view

Let's take a closer look at MYLETTER now.

1. Type **1** to get a 100% view, the actual size the document will be when it's printed (Figure 11.2).
2. Type **2** to get a 200% enlargement. Press the **Right** and **Left arrow keys** to scroll the page sideways.
3. Press **F7** or click the right mouse button to return to your document.

Note that you can't do any editing in the View Document screen, but if you don't like what you see, simply return to the editing screen to change the document before you print it.

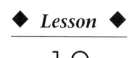

◆ *Lesson* ◆

12

Printing a Document

Now you're ready to print your letter. First, make sure your printer is turned on and that its "ready" light, if it has one, is on.

Printing the Letter

1. With the letter displayed on the editing screen, choose **Print** from the File menu or press **Shift-F7**. You'll see the Print menu again (Figure 12.1).
2. Type **f** for Full Document.
3. You'll see a "Please wait" message as WordPerfect sends the document to the printer, and then your letter should appear from the printer.

Other Print Options

Printing the document that's displayed on the screen in its entirety is only one of the ways you can print a document from WordPerfect. Refer to the Print menu again to see what some of your other print options are.

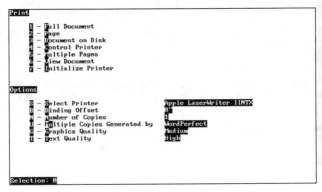

Figure 12.1   The Print menu

Choosing the Page option prints just the page that's displayed. In a long document this is a wise choice, especially if the document is not in its final form. You'll save time and paper by printing out individual pages if you think there's a problem instead of printing out the entire document.

Document on Disk lets you print a document that's *not* currently on the editing screen. If you know the document name, all you have to do is choose this option, enter the name, and then choose which pages you want to print. Press **Enter** at the "Page(s): All" prompt to print the whole document, or use the system shown in Table 12.1 to print selected pages.

The Multiple Pages option is for printing specific pages of the document that's on the screen, not several copies of each page, as you might think. To print selected pages, you indicate them by using the system shown in Table 12.1.

Table 12.1 Specifying Pages to Print

Example	Prints
Page(s): 8	Page 8 only
Page(s): 8, 15	Pages 8 and 15
Page(s): 8–9, 15	Pages 8 through 9 and page 15
Page(s): 15–	From page 15 to the end of the document
Page(s): –15	From the beginning of the document through page 15

Tip
You can also print a selected block of text from a page of a document just by highlighting it and choosing Print from the File menu. You'll be prompted, "Print block?" Type y for Yes. (You'll learn more about blocks of text in Lesson 17.)

Choosing a Different Printer

To select a different printer other than the one whose name is displayed on the Print menu next to Select Printer, type **s** for Select Printer to see a list of all the printers that are installed on your computer.

Printing More Than One Copy

To print several copies of a document, type **n** for Number of Copies and enter the quantity you want. The program is preset to print one copy.

Controlling the Printer

As each document is sent to the printer, it is placed in a line, called a queue. If documents aren't coming out of your printer as quickly as you think they should, or if you suspect some other problem, there's an easy way to determine what's happening: Choose Control Printer (Figure 12.2) by typing **c** when the Print menu is displayed. You'll see a screen showing which page is currently printing and any messages about problems such as, "Printer not accepting characters."

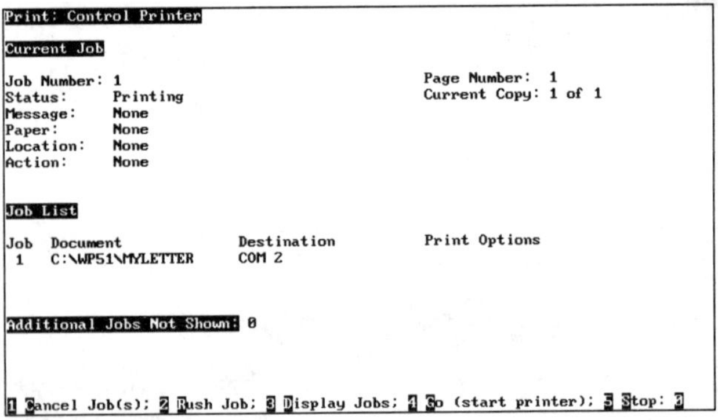

```
Print: Control Printer

Current Job

Job Number: 1                           Page Number:  1
Status:      Printing                   Current Copy: 1 of 1
Message:     None
Paper:       None
Location:    None
Action:      None

Job List

Job  Document              Destination        Print Options
 1   C:\WP51\MYLETTER      COM 2

Additional Jobs Not Shown: 0


1 Cancel Job(s); 2 Rush Job; 3 Display Jobs; 4 Go (start printer); 5 Stop: 0
```

Figure 12.2 The Control Printer screen

To Stop Printing

Sometimes you may need to stop printing because of a paper jam or some other problem that demands immediate attention. Here's how to do it:

1. Turn the printer off.
2. In WordPerfect, go to the Print menu, type **c** for Control Printer, and select **Cancel Job(s)**.
3. Type an asterisk (*****) to cancel all your print jobs.
4. Respond to the rest of the prompts you'll see about canceling all printing.

Now you can give the printer your attention.

Pausing the Printer

You also have the option to temporarily pause the printer without canceling printing. Instead of choosing Cancel, choose Stop. Your printer will probably print out another page or two, depending on how much of the document is already in the queue, but then it will stop. After you've fixed the problem, type **g** for Go to start printing again.

 Don't exit from WordPerfect while you're printing, unless you want to cancel all your print jobs.

◆ *Lesson* ◆

13

Editing Text

Because rarely, if ever, is anything created perfectly the first time, you have to know how to change and fix your documents. In this lesson we'll look at how easy it is to make changes in WordPerfect. You'll learn to delete words and blank lines, combine two paragraphs into one, and more.

Sample Text

First, you need to have some text on the screen to work with, so as with the sample letter, let's do some typing.

1. Start WordPerfect, if it's not already running.
2. Type these two short paragraphs (see Figure 13.1):

   It was good to hear from you last week, and I'm looking forward to our meeting.

   If you have any questions, give me a call at (408) 555-1278.

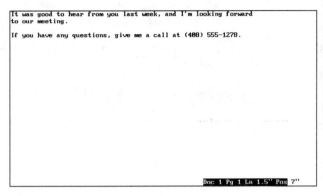

It was good to hear from you last week, and I'm looking forward
to our meeting.

If you have any questions, give me a call at (408) 555-1278.

Doc 1 Pg 1 Ln 1.5'' Pos 7''

Figure 13.1   Entering sample paragraphs

3. Press **Enter** twice after the first sentence to put a
blank line between paragraphs.

Deleting Words

You've already learned to delete characters by pressing
Backspace (to delete to the left of the cursor) and Del
(to delete to the right of the cursor). WordPerfect also
lets you delete whole words. Try this now:

1. Put the cursor anywhere in the word *good* in the
first sentence.

2. Press **Ctrl-Backspace** to delete the whole word.

You also can delete several words at one time by
combining WordPerfect's Repeat feature with the Ctrl-
Backspace key combination. Just press **Esc**, enter the
number of words you want to delete, and then press
Ctrl-Backspace once.

Undeleting

What if you change your mind and want to get back the word you just deleted? Easy.

1. Press **F1** (Cancel) or choose **Undelete** from the Edit menu. You'll see the word at the bottom of your screen along with two options: Restore and Previous Deletion (Figure 13.2).
2. Type **r** for Restore.

If you type **p** for Previous deletion, you'll see any deletion that was made before the last word you deleted. WordPerfect remembers the last three things you deleted, and you can undelete any of them. Type **p** twice to see the text that was deleted two steps earlier.

Figure 13.2 Undoing a deletion

Deleting a Line

When you want to delete a whole line at one time:

1. Put the cursor at the beginning of the line of text you want to delete. (Pressing **Home** and the **Left arrow** key will quickly move it to the beginning of the line.)
2. Press **Ctrl-End** to delete the whole line.
3. Press **F1** or choose **Undelete** from the Edit menu and type **r** to get the line back.

Note, if the cursor isn't at the beginning of a line, pressing Ctrl-End deletes only from the cursor's position to the end of that line.

Deleting a Blank Line

It's easy to delete blank lines, too.

1. Put the cursor at the beginning of the blank line between the two paragraphs in our sample text.
2. Press **Del**.

You'll see that the line of text below the blank line moved up one line when the blank was deleted (Figure 13.3).

Combining Two Paragraphs

Now that the blank line is deleted, all you have to do to combine the two paragraphs is press Del again to bring them together.

1. Make sure the cursor is at the space following the end of the first paragraph.

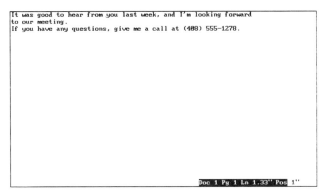

Figure 13.3 Deleting a blank line

2. Press **Del** to join the two sentences.
3. Press the **Spacebar** to put a space between the period and the first word of the next sentence.

Now you have only one paragraph of text, as shown in Figure 13.4.

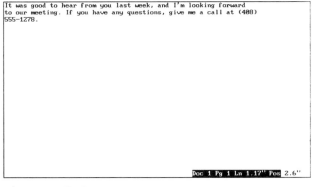

Figure 13.4 Joining paragraphs

Deleting Accidental Returns

As mentioned at the beginning of the book, it's hard to break the typewriter habit of pressing Enter at the end of each line. Fortunately, it's easy to correct this common mistake. First, though, let's make the mistake.

1. Move the cursor to the letter t in meeting.
2. Press **Enter** to break the line.
3. Press **Del** to correct the error and join the lines again.

What's actually happening when you split and join paragraphs is that invisible Hard Return [HRt] formatting codes are being inserted and deleted. You can view these codes at any time while you're working on a document. Just choose Reveal Codes from the Edit menu or press **Alt-F3**. (You'll learn more about these codes in Lesson 28.)

Keep the sample text on your screen for use in the next lesson.

14

Undoing More Mistakes

You saw in the last lesson how easy it is to retrieve text using WordPerfect's Undelete feature. Truthfully, if you've only deleted a few characters by mistake, it's probably faster to retype them than to use Undelete. The Undelete feature's real value becomes clear when you've deleted larger amounts of text—several sentences, paragraphs, or pages—that you must get back.

Deleting a Sentence, Paragraph, or Page

WordPerfect has a built-in feature that lets you select the current sentence, paragraph, or page. Let's see how this works.

1. Put the cursor anywhere in the first sentence of the sample text.
2. Choose **Select** from the Edit menu; then choose **Sentence**, or press **Ctrl-F4** and type **s**.

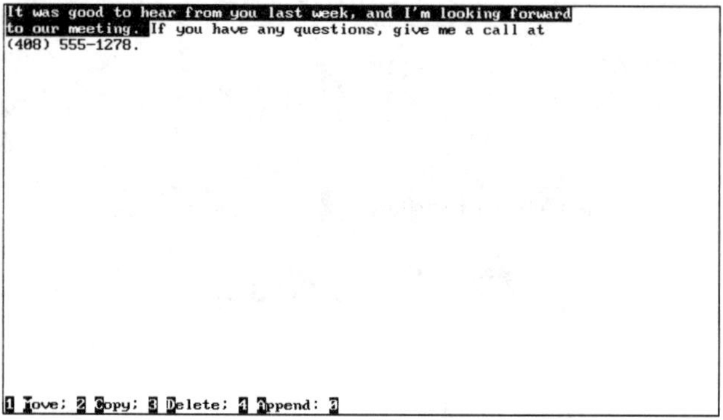

```
It was good to hear from you last week, and I'm looking forward
to our meeting. If you have any questions, give me a call at
(408) 555-1278.
```

```
1 Move; 2 Copy; 3 Delete; 4 Append: 3
```

Figure 14.1   Marking a sentence for deletion

3. The first sentence will be highlighted; type **d** for Delete, or press **Del** or **Backspace**, to delete it (Figure 14.1).
4. To restore the sentence you just deleted, press **F1** (or choose **Undelete** from the Edit menu) and type **r**.

Your other choices in this process, as you probably noticed in the steps above, are Move, Copy, and Append; Move and Copy are discussed in Lesson 17.

You can delete entire paragraphs and pages in this way, so it's easy to see how valuable the Undelete command can be.

Reversing Decisions

Remember that for some commands, F1 works as a Cancel or Undo key instead of as an Undelete key. You already know to press F1 to cancel an operation you're being prompted about, such as saving a document.

You also learned you can press F1 to back out of a menu without making any choices. WordPerfect automatically adjusts the response of the F1 key to either cancel an operation or undelete text.

Keep your sample text on the screen so that you're ready to search and replace in the next lesson.

◆ *Lesson* ◆

15

Searching and Replacing

One of WordPerfect's greatest timesaving features is that it lets you easily search for a word or phrase anywhere in your document. This can really be helpful if you're looking for a specific section in a long document or looking for information about a particular subject. It can also help you find the place where you left off when you were previously working in a document.

Tip

It's usually a good idea to start a search at the beginning of a document, to make sure that you've searched through the whole thing. Remember: WordPerfect searches just from the current cursor position to the end of the document (or to the beginning, if you search backward).

Searching

Although you've only got a short document to work with on the screen, it will illustrate how to use WordPerfect's Search capabilities. You can use your imagination to appreciate how much time this feature can save you in a long document.

1. Press **Home Home Up arrow** to go to the beginning of the document.
2. Select **Forward** from the Search menu or press **F2**. You'll see a "-> Srch:" prompt at the bottom of the screen (Figure 15.1).
3. Let's assume you're searching for the phone number in the sample text. Enter **555** and press **F2**.

Don't press Enter to start a search. This is a very common mistake made by beginners and veteran WordPerfect users alike. If you press Enter, WordPerfect assumes you want to search for one of those invisible [HRt] codes that indicate a hard return. Press F2 instead!

You're immediately taken to the 555 prefix of the phone number. Obviously, the speed isn't very impressive in this short document, but in a long document you'll be amazed and grateful at how fast it proceeds. And, searching is much, much faster than scrolling page by page!

Searching Again

If the first occurrence of the specified text the program locates isn't exactly what you're looking for, press **F2**

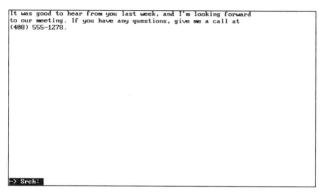

It was good to hear from you last week, and I'm looking forward
to our meeting. If you have any questions, give me a call at
(408) 555-1278.

→ Srch:

Figure 15.1 Starting a search

again to search for the next occurrence, or choose Next
or Previous from the Search menu.

To search for a different word or phrase, just type the
new item when you see the "-> Srch:" prompt. What
you type will replace what's already there.

Unsuccessful Searches

If WordPerfect doesn't find what you specified, the
message "* Not found *" will appear at the bottom of
the screen.

Searching Tips

You may enter as many as 59 characters in your search
string, including spaces. So, if you know you're looking
for a specific phrase, enter all of it. The more specific
you can be, the faster WordPerfect will find it.

Enter your search string in all lowercase letters, especially if you're not sure how it's capitalized in the

document. If you capitalize a word, WordPerfect will search only for words that match exactly; but, if you enter the word in lowercase letters, it will find the word no matter how or if it's capitalized.

To return to the beginning of the search, press **Ctrl-Home** twice.

Normally, WordPerfect searches only through the text of a document. You can search through everything, however, including footnotes, endnotes, headers, footers, captions—*everything*. Just choose **Extended Search** from the Search menu or press **Home** before you press **F2**.

Searching and Replacing

Another great timesaver is that WordPerfect lets you search for a word or phrase and replace it with something entirely different at the same time. Think for a minute about how much work this can save you. Say that you're writing a story whose main character is named George. You decide for some reason that you'd like to rename George *Joe*, even though his name appears in maybe one hundred places in the story. Well, you don't have to search for each George and manually change it to Joe. Follow these steps to search *and* replace:

1. Return to the top of the document with **Home Home Up arrow**. Let's change every occurrence of the word *you* to *Joe*.
2. Choose **Replace** from the Search menu or press **Alt-F2**.
3. Type **y** to confirm each replacement.

Confirm replacements as they're being made, unless you're *absolutely* sure that you want to change everything all at once. It's very easy to make a mistake and replace parts of words without even realizing it, because the program will do *exactly* what you tell it to. If you tell it to replace *black* with *white*, it will do that, but it will include any words in which black is only a part, so you'll get words like *whitened* (instead of *blackened*), *whiteberries* instead of *blackberries*, and even *white*-eyed peas. You can avoid this problem another way—replace whole words and not just parts of words. Press the Spacebar at the end of the search word when you enter it at the "search for" and "replace with" prompts.

4. At the search prompt, type **you** and press **F2**.

5. At the replace with: prompt, type **Joe** then **F2**.

6. The program will stop at the first *you* and ask whether to change it (Figure 15.2). Type **y** for Yes.

---

t was good to hear from you last week, and I'm looking forward
to our meeting. If you have any questions, give me a call at
(408) 555-1278.

Confirm? No (Yes)   Doc 1 Pg 1 Ln 1" Pos 3.6"

Figure 15.2   Searching and replacing

7. It then goes to the next *you* and asks whether that one should be replaced. That wouldn't make much sense, so type **n** for No.

Tip
It's a good idea to save a document just before you start a Search and Replace operation. That way, if you do create unusual words by mistake, you can retrieve the saved document and start the procedure again.

Now that you've seen how searching and replacing work, let's look at another wonderful WordPerfect feature, Speller.

♦ *Lesson* ♦

16
The Speller

One feature you'll love in WordPerfect is its excellent spelling checker. It seems that no matter how badly you mistype a word, the Speller can figure out what you really meant and suggest the right word for you.

It's recommended that you get in the habit of running the Speller on each document when you finish it to ensure that you catch all the typographical errors *before* you take the document out of the printer.

Running the Speller

Again, you'll need some text to spell check, so clear the screen and retrieve MYLETTER. You'll recall that you inserted some deliberate mistakes in it for the explicit purpose of learning to use the Speller.

1. Choose the **Spell** option from the Tools menu or press **Ctrl-F2**.
2. Type **d** for Document in order to check the whole document.

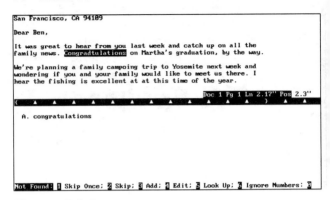

San Francisco, CA 94109

Dear Ben,

It was great to hear from you last week and catch up on all the
family news. Congradtulations on Martha's graduation, by the way.

We're planning a family camping trip to Yosemite next week and
wondering if you and your family would like to meet us there. I
hear the fishing is excellent at at this time of the year.

```
                                        Doc 1 Pg 1 Ln 2.17" Pos 2.3"
{   ▲    ▲    ▲    ▲    ▲    ▲    ▲    ▲    ▲   ▲    ▲    ▲    }   ▲    ▲
```

  A. congratulations

```
Not Found: 1 Skip Once; 2 Skip; 3 Add; 4 Edit; 5 Look Up; 6 Ignore Numbers: 7
```

Figure 16.1 Suggesting a replacement

Tip
You can check just the current page instead of
the whole document. This is often useful in a
long document where you've just revised a paragraph or two of text on a page.

3. When the Speller starts, the program shows suggested replacements in the lower half of the
   screen (Figure 16.1). It stopped first on *Congradtulations* and is suggesting the correct word,
   congratulations.
4. Type **a** to accept the replacement. Notice that the
   program automatically matches the capitalization of the word it found.
5. Next the Speller stopped on *campoing* (Figure
   16.2). You could type **a** to replace it with *camping*,
   but let's see how editing the word works.

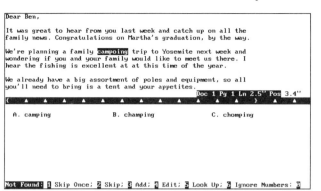

```
Dear Ben,

It was great to hear from you last week and catch up on all the
family news. Congratulations on Martha's graduation, by the way.

We're planning a family campoing trip to Yosemite next week and
wondering if you and your family would like to meet us there. I
hear the fishing is excellent at at this time of the year.

We already have a big assortment of poles and equipment, so all
you'll need to bring is a tent and your appetites.
                                            Doc 1 Pg 1 Ln 2.5" Pos 3.4"
(   ▲   ▲   ▲   ▲   ▲   ▲   ▲   ▲   ▲   ▲   ▲   }   ▲   ▲

   A. camping           B. champing           C. chomping




Not Found: 1 Skip Once; 2 Skip; 3 Add; 4 Edit; 5 Look Up; 6 Ignore Numbers: 0
```

Figure 16.2   Querying another word

6. Press the **Right arrow** key 5 times to move to
   the *o* in *campoing*. Then press **Del** to delete it.

> **Tip**
>
> Although there's an Edit option on the menu,
> you don't have to use it. Just press the Right
> arrow key to edit a word in the document.

7. Press **Enter** to start the Speller again.
8. The Speller stops at the double word *at at* (Figure
   16.3). This is a mistake too, so type **3** to delete the
   second *at*.
9. The Speller stops again, this time on *Thursady*
   (Figure 16.4). Type **a** to replace it with the correct
   spelling.

The Speller continues to check the rest of the document. It may find more mistakes than these, depending on how accurately you typed, but these examples
show you the basics of how it works.

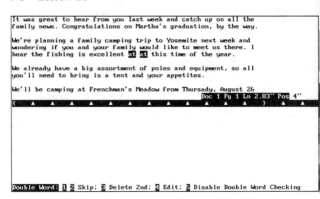

Figure 16.3 Checking a double word

When the spell check is complete, you'll see the number of words that it queried in the document.

 Be sure to save your document after you run the Speller. WordPerfect doesn't automatically save the corrected version.

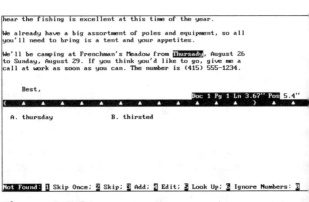

Figure 16.4 Spell check continues

Skipping Words

If the Speller queries you on a word that you want to leave as it's typed, (often the name of a person or company) type **1** for Skip Once or **2** for Skip. If you choose Skip Once and the Speller runs across the same word later in the document, it will stop at it again. If you choose Skip, the Speller ignores the word in the rest of the document.

Adding Words

There undoubtedly will be words that you want to add to the Speller's dictionary so it will stop asking you about them, like your Uncle Zolliecofer's name or a city name it doesn't know. To add a word that the Speller is querying, choose option 3, Add.

Ignoring Numbers

The Speller normally stops at any combination of letters and numbers. If you often type documents with entries such as "the F1 function key," choose option 6, Ignore Numbers, early in your session with the Speller so that it won't ask you about letter-number combinations.

Looking Up a Word

You may on occasion want to check the spelling of just one word. Let's see how that works.

1. Start the Speller again. Choose **Spell** from the Tools menu or press **Ctrl-F2**.

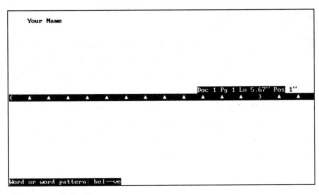

Figure 16.5   Looking up a word

2. This time, type **5** for Look Up. You'll see the screen shown in Figure 16.5.
3. Perhaps you're not sure how *believe* is spelled; is it *ei* or *ie?* Type **bel--ve** and press **Enter**. The Speller will suggest replacements (Figure 16.6).

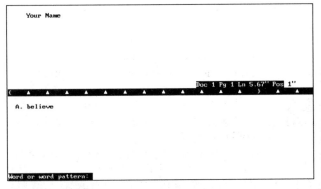

Figure 16.6   Getting the right spelling

Tip

If you have no idea how a word is spelled, use an asterisk (*) to represent the parts you don't know. For example, if you entered re*ve, Word-Perfect would return a long list of correctly spelled words that start with *re* and end in *ve*, like *receive* and *recessive*. You can even try phonetic spelling—entering imaginashun will, for example, get you *imagination*.

Checking Capitalization

The Speller also checks for irregular capitalization. This is a great help when you unknowingly type words like LIst instead of List. When the Speller finds a word like this, it will ask you about it, too.

Exiting from the Speller

If you want to stop the spell-checking process before it's complete, press F1, the Cancel key. (You may have to press it more than once to return to your document.) Then, remember to save the document if you want to save all the corrections you made up to that point.

While the Speller can find typographical errors and suggest replacements for them, it has no way of knowing if you've typed the wrong word. If, for example, you type *it's* when you mean *its*, or *your* when you wanted *you're*, the Speller won't query you about those words. So, you still must proofread your document carefully.

◆ *Lesson* ◆

17

Working with Blocks of Text

Several of WordPerfect's commands can be carried out on blocks of text, all at once. This too is a great timesaver. Instead of working with one character or word at a time, once you've selected a block of text, you can:

- Delete it
- Copy it
- Move it
- Make it **boldface** or underline it
- Change its font
- Change its alignment
- Convert it to uppercase or lowercase
- Spell check it
- Save it as a separate file
- Append it to the end of another file

The first three of these capabilities—deleting, copying, and moving—are covered in this lesson.

Selecting Text

Either continue to work on MYLETTER or retrieve a different document so you can practice selecting blocks of text, using the methods described in this section.

There are three different ways to select text:

1. With a mouse, the easiest way to select text is to drag over it, holding the left mouse button down.
2. Without a mouse, choose **Block** from the Edit menu and then use the arrow keys to highlight the text you want.
3. Press **Alt-F4** to turn on block marking; then use the arrow keys to highlight text.

No matter which method you use, you'll see a flashing "Block on" prompt at the bottom left-hand corner of the screen, indicating that you can mark a block of text (Figure 17.1).

```
Benjamin Jefferson
2100 Water St.
San Francisco, CA 94109

Dear Ben,

It was great to hear from you last week and catch up on all the
family news. Congratulations on Martha's graduation, by the way.

We're planning a family camping trip to Yosemite next week and
wondering if you and your family would like to meet us there. I
hear the fishing is excellent at this time of the year.

We already have a big assortment of poles and equipment, so all
you'll need to bring is a tent and your appetites.

We'll be camping at Frenchman's Meadow from Thursday, August 26
to Sunday, August 29. If you think you'd like to go, give me a
call at work as soon as you can. The number is (415) 555-1234.

     Best,

Block on                          Doc 1 Pg 1 Ln 1.5" Pos 1"
```

Figure 17.1 Marking a block of text

Canceling a Selection

If you change your mind and want to turn the high-lighting off before you do anything with the block of text, click the left mouse button again, or press **F1** (Cancel), or type **Alt-F4** again.

Deleting a Block of Text

Once you've highlighted a block of text, all you need to do to delete it is press the **Del** or **Backspace** key. You'll be asked if this is really what you want to do; for now, type **y** for Yes.

Remember from Lessons 13 and 14 that you retrieve text you mistakenly delete by choosing Undelete from the Edit menu or pressing the F1 Cancel key.

Moving (Cutting) a Block of Text

It's so easy to reorganize text in WordPerfect: All you need to do to move text around is mark it as a block, choose Move, move it to another spot in the document, and press Enter. Try it now:

1. Highlight a block of text in your practice document. Then choose **Move** from the Edit menu, or use the keyboard shortcut **Ctrl-Del**. (You can also press **Ctrl-F4**, choose **Block**, and then choose **Move**, but the keyboard shortcut is faster.)
2. The text disappears, and the message "Move cursor; press Enter to retrieve" appears.
3. Move the cursor to the place where you want the cut text to go. Then press **Enter**, and the text appears in that place.

Think of the process of moving text as first cutting it and then pasting it in a new location. If you want to cut it to eliminate it, press **F1** while the "Move cursor; press Enter to retrieve" message is displayed. Be aware, however, that unlike text you delete (by using the Del or Backspace keys), text you cut cannot be restored with WordPerfect's Undelete feature. You can get cut text back, though. Press **Shift-F10** or choose **Retrieve** from the File menu; then press **Enter** to restore the text you cut.

Copying a Block

Copying text that must appear in more than one place in a document can save you a lot of retyping. This process works like moving (cutting) text, except that the text stays in its original position and a copy of it also appears where indicated when you press Enter. Here are the steps to follow:

1. Mark a block of text in your practice document. Then choose **Copy** from the Edit menu or press **Ctrl-Ins**.
2. You'll see the "Move cursor; press Enter to retrieve" prompt again. Move the cursor to the position at which you want the copied text to go, and then press **Enter** to see the copy appear.

If you don't select any text before you begin the Copy procedure, WordPerfect assumes that you want to move or copy either a complete sentence, a whole paragraph, or a full page. If, in fact, this is what you want to do, you don't have to mark it first. Just press **Ctrl-F4** or choose **Select** from the Edit menu and then pick **Sentence**, **Paragraph**, or **Page** to select the appropriate one.

Keep your document on the screen to practice changing margins in the next lesson.

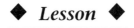

◆ *Lesson* ◆

18

Setting Document Margins

WordPerfect has a default margin setting of one inch all around—top, bottom, left, and right. If you're printing on plain paper without any letterhead, these settings will serve you well. But to accommodate letterheads or special looks you want to achieve, you'll need to know how to change margin settings.

Top and Bottom Margins

If you're printing on letterhead that has text at the top of the sheet (perhaps the bottom, too), you will no doubt need to change the top and bottom margins. Here's how to do it.

1. Measure from the top edge of the paper to where you want the new margin to begin. Let's assume for this exercise you want 2.5 inches instead of 1 inch to allow for the letterhead.
2. Go to the beginning of the document (press **Home Home Up arrow**).

```
Format: Page

    1 - Center Page (top to bottom)        No

    2 - Force Odd/Even Page

    3 - Headers

    4 - Footers

    5 - Margins - Top                      1"
                  Bottom                   1"

    6 - Page Numbering

    7 - Paper Size                         8.5" x 11"
             Type                          Standard
             Labels

    8 - Suppress (this page only)



Selection: 0
```

Figure 18.1   The Page Format menu

3. Choose **Page** from the Layout menu or press **Shift-F8** and type **p** for Page. You'll see the Page Format menu (Figure 18.1).
4. Type **m** for Margins.
5. Enter the new number for the top margin—in this case, **2.5**. (The program assumes you're entering measurements in inches.) Then press **Enter**. If you want to set a new bottom margin, type its size and press **Enter**.
6. Press **F7** to return to your document.

Note that you won't be able to see the effects of the procedure above on the editing screen. To see how the document looks, use the View Document feature that you were introduced to in Lesson 11.

 All the pages in your document will now have a 2.5-inch top margin unless you reset the margin again.

Tip

You can make room for just one sheet with a preprinted letterhead without resetting the top margin for the entire document. Just press Enter until the cursor is at the Ln 2.5" mark. Check the status line to see the cursor's position.

Right and Left Margins

To reset right and left margins, you take the same steps as setting top and bottom margins, except that you choose **Line** from the Layout menu or press **Shift-F8** and type **l** for Line.

1. Measure from the left edge of the paper to where you want the new margin to begin—say, 3 inches instead of 1 inch, to leave room for handwritten notes.
2. To reset the margins for the whole document, go to the beginning of the document (press **Home Home Up arrow**).
3. Choose **Line** from the Layout menu or press **Shift-F8** and type **l** for Line. You'll see the Line Format menu (Figure 18.2).
4. Type **m** for Margins.
5. Enter the new number for the left margin—in this case, **3**. Then press **Enter**. If you want to set a new right margin, type its size (measured from the right edge of the paper) and press **Enter**.
6. Press **F7** to return to your document.

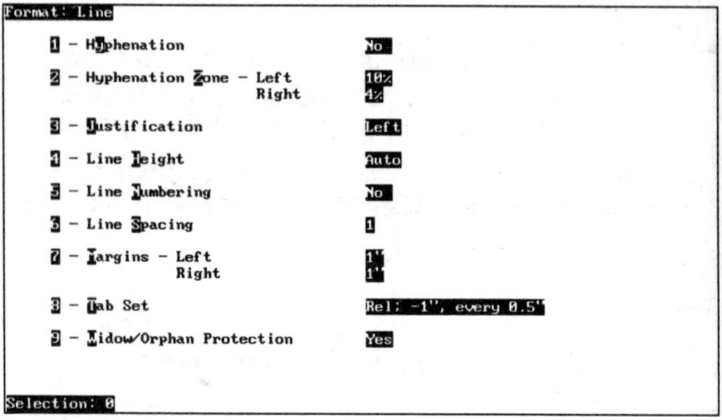

Format: Line
```
    1 – Hyphenation                          No
    2 – Hyphenation Zone – Left              10%
                          Right              4%
    3 – Justification                        Left
    4 – Line Height                          Auto
    5 – Line Numbering                       No
    6 – Line Spacing                         1
    7 – Margins – Left                       1"
                  Right                      1"
    8 – Tab Set                              Rel; -1", every 0.5"
    9 – Widow/Orphan Protection              Yes
```
Selection: 0

Figure 18.2   The Line Format menu

Various Margins within a Document

Sometimes you may want to reset margins for just part of a document. To do this, just put the cursor where you want the margins to change and then reset them. The new settings will stay in effect until you set margins again.

Not Getting the Right Margins?

If you've reset margins but the new settings are not reflected in the printed document, the invisible codes may be the culprit. WordPerfect reads the margin setting that's nearest the cursor, and it may not be the one you want. To find out if this is the case, open the Reveal Codes window and check the codes.

1. Choose **Reveal Codes** from the Edit menu or press **Alt-F3**. You'll see a screen like the one in

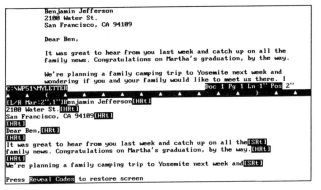

Figure 18.3 Locating margin codes

Figure 18.3. (The code for left and right margin
changes is [L/R Mar:] followed by the settings and
[T/B Mar:] plus those settings for top and bottom
margins.)

2. Use the arrow keys to highlight the margin setting you don't want. Press **Del** to remove it.
3. Reset the margins to the settings you want.

Centering a Page Vertically

WordPerfect has a built-in Center Page feature that will
center text vertically on a page, which means you
don't have to measure margins and reset them. It's
especially handy for one-page business letters or short
memos, because you don't have to do anything except
choose the command.

1. Go to the beginning of the letter or memo
   (**Home Home Up arrow**).
2. Choose **Page** from the Layout menu or press
   Shift-F8 and type **p** for Page.

3. Type **c** for Center Page (top to bottom).
4. Type **y** for Yes.
5. Press **F7** to return to your document.

Again, you won't see the results on the editing screen, but if you use the View Document feature, you'll see that the program automatically calculated new top and bottom margins and adjusted them so that the text is centered on the page. This feature affects only the top and bottom margins, not the right and left margins.

◆ *Lesson* ◆

19

Setting Tabs

Many people, when they first start using a word processing program on a computer, try to align text or indent paragraphs by using the Spacebar. Don't. Use the Tab key instead.

If you use the Spacebar to insert spaces, you'll get different increments of space each time you change typefaces because every font has a different space size. Everything may look just fine on your screen, but when you print, text won't be indented and aligned consistently. The characters that appear on the screen aren't the same characters you're going to get when you print.

With that warning in mind, let's continue to learn how to use tabs. They are indispensible for aligning text in columns, typing numbers that align on the decimal point, or even for typing text with dot leaders. Look at the examples in Figure 19.1. Then look at Figure 19.2, which shows some sample information that's formatted by setting tabs.

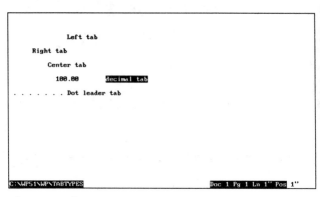

Figure 19.1 Tab alignments

⇨ **Note:** If the information you're typing is much longer or more complex than what's shown in Figure 19.2, it's more efficient to use WordPerfect's Tables feature instead of setting columns with tabs. Tabs are best used for short columns of simple data.

Course	Number	Grade Average
History	2-25	3.5
Geometry	40-01	4.5
English	10-8	2.75

Figure 19.2 A sample table created with tabs

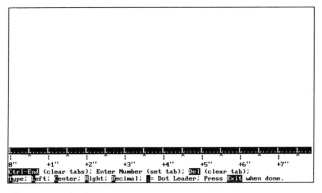

Figure 19.3 The tab ruler

Setting a Tab

There is one general method for setting tabs, no matter which type of tab you want to set:

1. Choose **Line** from the Layout menu or press **Shift-F8** and type **l** for Line.
2. Type **t** for Tab Set. You'll see the tab ruler (Figure 19.3) on the screen.
3. Use the arrow keys to move the cursor to the tab location. Then type **l** for a left-aligned tab, **r** for a right-aligned tab, **c** for a centered tab, or **d** for a decimal tab. If you want a tab with a dot leader, type a period before you type the letter.

Tip

As soon as you see the tab ruler, press Ctrl-End to delete all existing tab settings so that you don't get confused about which ones the program set and which ones you set.

4. To delete a tab, move the cursor to it and then press **Del**.
5. When you're though setting tabs, press **F7** twice to return to your document to type.

An Example

We'll recreate the columns shown in Figure 19.2 so you can practice setting right, left, and decimal tabs, as well as centering headings over columns. Open a new document so you can follow along.

1. At the beginning of the document, choose **Line** from the Layout menu or press **Shift-F8** and type **l** for Line.
2. Type **t** for Tab Set.
3. Press **Ctrl-End** to delete all current tab settings.
4. Press the **Right arrow** key to move the cursor to the +1" position.
5. Type **l** to insert a left tab.
6. Move the cursor to the +3" position.
7. Type **r** to insert a right tab.
8. Move to the 4.5" position.
9. Type **d** to insert a decimal tab.
10. Your screen should look like Figure 19.4. Press **F7** twice to return to your document.

Next you'll type the headings. The first heading stays left-aligned, the second is right-aligned, and the third is centered over the column.

1. Press **Tab** and type **Course**.
2. Press **Tab** and type **Number.**

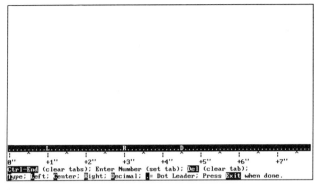

Figure 19.4 Setting tabs

3. Press **Tab** and then press **Shift-F6** to center the next heading. WordPerfect centers a heading over a tab setting if you press Shift-F6 after you press Tab. (You can also choose **Align** from the Layout menu and then select **Center**.) Then type your heading.
4. Type **Grade Average**.
5. Press **Enter** twice to insert a blank line.

The next step is to enter the text for the columns.

1. Press **Tab** and type **History**.
2. Press **Tab** and type **2-25**.
3. Press **Tab** and type **3.5**. You'll see the message "Align Char = ." at the bottom of the screen. This means that the numbers will align on the decimal point (period), which is what you want, because you've set a decimal tab there.

Tip

Set decimal tabs if you're typing columns of dollars and cents. The numbers will align correctly on the decimal point when you're done. They may look strange as you're typing them, because they won't align until you type the period.

4. Press **Enter** to go to the next line.
5. Press **Tab**, type **Geometry**, press **Tab**, type **40-01**, press **Tab**, and type **4.5**.
6. Press **Enter** to go to the next line.
7. Press **Tab**, type **English**, press **Tab**, type **18-8**, press **Tab**, and type **2.75**.

When you're finished typing, your screen should resemble Figure 19.2.

Resetting Tabs

Once you have finished with a format that calls for several tabs, you'll probably want to reset the tabs back to every half-inch (the WordPerfect default). If you don't, the ones you set for the columnar material will stay in effect, which is probably not what you want if you'll be working with normal paragraph text again. To reset tabs:

1. Choose **Line** from the Layout menu or press **Shift-F8** and type **l** for Line.
2. Type **t** for Tab Set.

3. Type **0.5** and press **Enter**. This sets tabs to evenly spaced half-inch intervals (see "Setting Evenly Spaced Tabs" below).

4. Press **F7** twice to return to your document.

Setting Evenly Spaced Tabs

If you want to set tabs at evenly spaced intervals—say, at every inch instead of every half inch—you can have the program calculate the spacing for you.

All you need to do is display the tab ruler, type the position (in inches) where you want the tabs to start, then type a comma; finally, type the increment you want the tabs to be spaced apart. To set tabs at every inch after the 2-inch mark you'd type **2,1**.

When to Use Tabs?

In general, tabs and the Tab key should be used to type small amounts of words and numbers that need to be aligned. For large amounts of text that will appear in rows and columns, you'll find it easier to use the Word-Perfect Tables feature. And for aligning lines of text in paragraphs, it's easier to change the justification than to use tabs, as you'll see in the next lesson.

20
Aligning Text

WordPerfect normally uses full justification on lines of text, which means that when your document is printed, text aligns at both the right and left margins, like the text you see in this book. As with other Word-Perfect features already discussed, this justification is not reflected on the editing screen, but does take effect when you print a document or use the View Document feature to preview it.

Left Alignment

A lot of people prefer a more informal look to their documents, with the text aligned on the left but not on the right; this is as you see it on the screen. Either way is fine: it's simply a matter of which style you prefer.

Note: With left justification, you won't get inconsistent spacing between words and letters that usually occurs with full justification, which happens because the program must align the text on both margins, regardless how many characters there are on a line. Therefore, a line with less text will appear more "spaced out" when printed.

To switch the alignment to left justification, also called ragged right:

1. To make sure that the change affects the whole document, go to the top of the document before you change justification. (Press **Home Home Up arrow**.)
2. Choose **Justify** from the Layout menu and then choose **Left**, or press **Shift-F8** and type **l** for Line and **j** for Justification.
3. Type **l** for Left justification.
4. Press **F7** to return to your document.

If you want to switch to left justification for all the documents you create, there's an easy way to do that. You'll find out how in Lesson 29.

Center Justification

Center justification is ideal for text that you want to center between the margins for a "displayed" look (see Figure 20.1), such as headlines, quotations, or important points.

The steps you take to use center justification are the same as for left justification, except you choose Center instead of Left. To return to regular full or left justification after you've typed the lines you want to be centered, take the same steps again, this time choosing Full or Left justification.

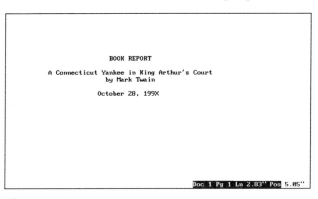

Figure 20.1 Using center justification

Centering a Line or Two of Text

When you turn on center justification, all the text you type will be centered until you change the justification again. Therefore, if you want to center just a line or two of text, it's faster to use the Align command, because as soon as you press Enter, center alignment is turned off and the alignment you've chosen for the body of the document again takes effect.

Let's see how this works. Clear the screen so you can see clearly what's happening.

1. Choose **Align** from the Layout menu; then choose **Center**. (Or you can bypass the menu system by pressing **Shift-F6** for Center.)
2. Type a few words and see how they are centered.
3. Press **Enter**; then type a few more words. They'll appear at the left margin.

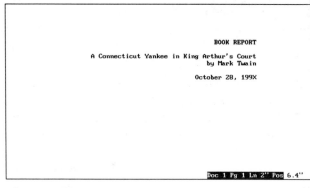

Figure 20.2   Using right justification

Right Justification

Right justification, too, can create a special effect in your documents. See Figure 20.2 for an example of how it looks. You'll often see it used in the closing of letters or for the attribution of quotations.

Turn on right justification in exactly the same way as the other types of justification, except choose Right instead of Full, Left, or Center.

Tip

To right justify just one line of text at a time, press Alt-F6 and type the text instead of turning right justification on and off.

Aligning a Block of Text

You can mark a block of text and then align the lines within it. If there are several lines you want to align together, use this method. It's faster than aligning one line at a time, and it's easier than turning justification on and then off.

1. Mark the text as a block.
2. Choose **Align** from the Layout menu.
3. Choose **Center** or **Flush Right**, or press **Shift-F6** or **Alt-F6**.
4. You'll see the prompt "[Just:Center]?" or "[Just:Right]?," depending on which command you're using. Type **y** for Yes.

In the next lesson you will learn some other ways to indent text.

◆ *Lesson* ◆

21

Indenting Text

As you've already learned, it's easy to indent the first line of every paragraph: just press the Tab key. WordPerfect's default tab setting of every half inch is usually fine; but, for tabs that indent, you also can change that half-inch tab setting if you like, as you learned in Lesson 19.

But what if you want to indent all the lines in a paragraph? This is where WordPerfect's Indent feature is used, as you'll discover in this lesson.

Indenting Entire Paragraphs

To see how this works, clear the screen in order to follow along.

1. Type these two short paragraphs:

A good word processing program can save you a great deal of time, because you can edit documents without retyping them.

Press **Enter** twice to end the first paragraph and put a blank line between it and the next paragraph.

Learning to use WordPerfect is a smart choice, because you can exchange documents with just about everybody.

2. Now move the cursor to the beginning of the first paragraph. Choose **Align** from the Layout menu; then choose **Indent** or press **F4**, the keyboard shortcut.

The entire first paragraph indents one tab stop, as shown in Figure 21.1.

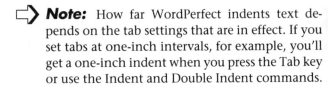 **Note:** How far WordPerfect indents text depends on the tab settings that are in effect. If you set tabs at one-inch intervals, for example, you'll get a one-inch indent when you press the Tab key or use the Indent and Double Indent commands.

You may choose Indent before or after you type a paragraph, but you must be at the beginning of the paragraph when you choose it.

 Tip

Using the Indent command is great for typing numbered lists. Type the number and a period (such as 1.). Then press F4 (Indent). Now all the lines will be neatly indented until you press Enter and type 2.; then press F4 again.

A good word processing proram can save you a great deal of
time, because you can edit documents without retyping them.

Learning to use WordPerfect is a smart choice, because you can
exchange documents with just about everybody.

C:\WP51\WP\FIG21-1   Doc 1 Pg 1 Ln 1" Pos 1"

Figure 21.1 Indenting a paragraph

Double Indents

WordPerfect also has a built-in double indent feature
(called Left/Right Indent) that's useful for displaying
paragraphs centered between the right and left margins. Let's see how this works.

1. Move the cursor to the beginning of the second
   paragraph in your document.
2. Choose **Align** from the Layout menu; then
   choose **Indent ->‹-** or press **Shift-F4**, the keyboard shortcut.

The second paragraph indents equally from the right
and left margins. Pressing Shift-F4 again will show the
effects even more clearly, as illustrated in Figure 21.2.
Double indents are often used to display quotations.

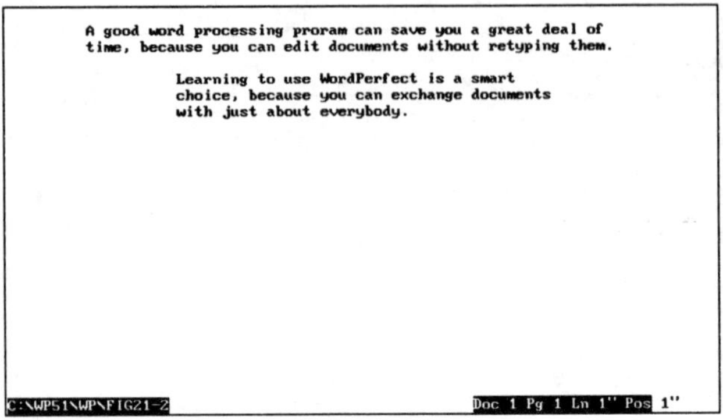

A good word processing proram can save you a great deal of time, because you can edit documents without retyping them.

Learning to use WordPerfect is a smart choice, because you can exchange documents with just about everybody.

C:\WP51\WP\FIG21-2   Doc 1 Pg 1 Ln 1" Pos 1"

Figure 21.2   Using a double indent

Hanging Indents

There's one other kind of indent that's useful to know how to create. Called the *hanging indent*, this format is often used in bibliographies and lists. Figure 21.3

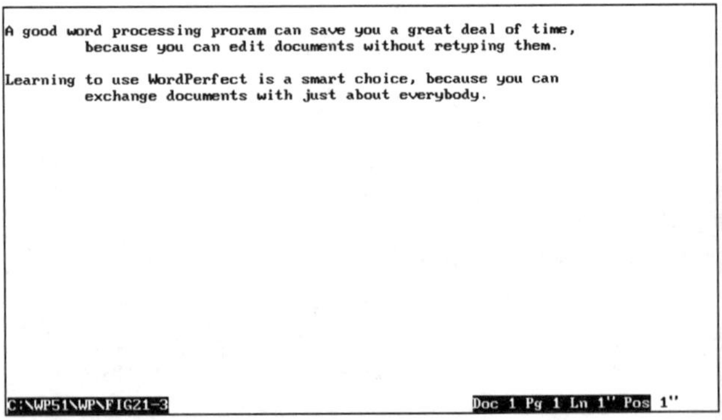

A good word processing proram can save you a great deal of time, because you can edit documents without retyping them.

Learning to use WordPerfect is a smart choice, because you can exchange documents with just about everybody.

C:\WP51\WP\FIG21-3   Doc 1 Pg 1 Ln 1" Pos 1"

Figure 21.3   Hanging indents

shows an example of hanging indents. To create a hanging indent:

1. At the beginning of the paragraph, choose **Align** from the Layout menu; then choose **Indent** (or press **F4**).

2. Now choose **Align** from the Layout menu and choose **Mar Rel** (Margin Release) (or press **Shift-Tab**).

The first Indent command indents the paragraph, and the Margin Release command moves the first line back to the previous tab setting.

◆ *Lesson* ◆

22

Setting and Changing Line Spacing

The WordPerfect default line spacing is single space, but many people find it easier to work with lines set double spaced, or more; lines separated by spaces are easier to read and edit. To change the line spacing, you could press Enter to insert blank lines. For one or two lines, that's acceptable, as you've seen throughout the exercises in this book. But for an entire document, it's a waste of your time and WordPerfect's capabilities.

Switching to Double Spacing

If you still have the two sample paragraphs from the previous lesson on the screen, you can use them for this example. If not, retrieve any other document to see how to change line spacing. At the beginning of the document:

1. Choose **Line** from the Layout menu. Then type **s** for Line Spacing. (You can press **Shift-F8** and type **l** and then **s** for a shortcut.)

135

2. Type **2** for double spacing. Then press **Enter**. (If you want space-and-a-half, type **1.5**; for triple spacing, type **3**.)
3. Press **F7** to return to your document.

The sample paragraphs are now double spaced as you can see in Figure 22.1. Notice the extra space between the two paragraphs. Where there was one blank line, there are now two.

Tip

To change the line spacing for the whole document, go to the beginning of the document first (Home Home Up arrow).

A good word processing proram can save you a great deal of time,

        because you can edit documents without retyping them.

Learning to use WordPerfect is a smart choice, because you can

        exchange documents with just about everybody.

C:\WP51\WP\FIG22-1   Doc 1 Pg 1 Ln 1" Pos 1"

Figure 22.1   Double spacing

Changing Spacing for a Paragraph or Two

You can change the spacing in just part of a document, too; the change takes effect from the position of the cursor onward. So, to switch to double spacing for a paragraph or two, put the cursor at the point where you want double spacing to begin. Then turn on double spacing exactly as in the steps above. Then move to where you want double spacing to end and turn on single spacing by repeating those steps again, this time typing **1**.

23

Page Numbers, Headers, and Footers

WordPerfect is preset *not* to number pages. Although you see "Pg" and a number on the status line, your printed documents won't have numbered pages unless you turn page numbering on.

Numbering Pages

Go to the beginning of the document if you want all the pages numbered; otherwise, WordPerfect starts numbering pages on the current page.

1. Choose **Page** from the Layout menu, or press **Shift-F8** and type **p** for Page. Then type **n** for Page Numbering. You'll see what the screen looks like in Figure 23.1.
2. Type **p** for Page Number Position. You'll see a display of where page numbers will appear if you type the number corresponding to that position (Figure 23.2). For example, type **7** to have page

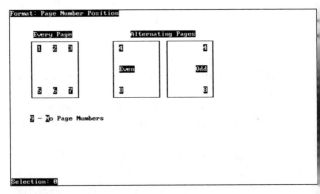

```
Format: Page Numbering
    1 - New Page Number         1
    2 - Page Number Style       ^B
    3 - Insert Page Number
    4 - Page Number Position    No page numbering




Selection: 0
```

Figure 23.1 The Page Numbering menu

numbers appear on every page in the bottom right-hand corner.

3. Press **F7** to return to your document.

Use the View Document feature (**Shift-F7 v**) to see the actual page numbers in position on the page.

```
Format: Page Number Position
        Every Page                  Alternating Pages
    1    2    3              4                      4

                            Even                   Odd

    5    6    7              8                      8

    9 - No Page Numbers



Selection: 0
```

Figure 23.2 Choosing page number position

Headers and Footers

Headers are text that appears at the top of every page; conversely, *footers* are text that appears at the bottom. Used typically in documents longer than one page, they usually contain information such as a report name, a chapter title, and page numbers.

 If you include page numbers in either your headers or footers, don't turn on page numbering, too. If you do, you'll end up with page numbers in two places!

Creating a Footer

You create headers and footers in exactly the same way—except, of course, you choose Header instead of Footer and vice versa. Clear the screen. In this exercise, we'll create a footer that appears on every page. It will read:

Chapter Two   Page *n*

When your document is printed, the *n* will be replaced by the actual page number.

1. Choose **Page** from the Format menu (or press **Shift-F8** and type **p** for Page). Then type **f** for Footer.
2. Type **a** for Footer A. (You may set up two different footers—Footer A for even pages and Footer B for odd pages, for example.)
3. Type **p** for Every Page. You'll see the footer editing screen, shown in Figure 23.3, which is where you type the actual text that will appear in the footer.

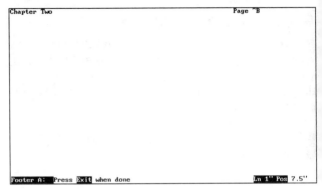

Figure 23.3   The footer editing screen

  4. Type **Chapter Two**.
  5. Press **Alt-F6** (Flush Right).
  6. Type **Page** and press the **Spacebar**.
  7. Press **Ctrl-B** to insert a ^B character, which tells
        WordPerfect to insert the page number.
  8. Press **F7** twice to turn to the document. Again,
        you won't see anything on the screen; headers
        and footers show up only in the View Docu-
        ment window and on the printed page.
  9. Press **Shift-F7** and type **v** to access the View
        Document screen. Your footer will be at the
        bottom of the page (Figure 23.4).
 10. Press **F7** to return to your document.

Editing Headers and Footers

If you change your mind about what's in the header or
footer, it's easy to edit it.

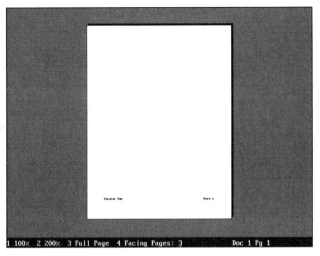

1 100% 2 200% 3 Full Page 4 Facing Pages: 3   Doc 1 Pg 1

Figure 23.4 Viewing the footer

1. Choose **Page** from the Format menu (or press **Shift-F8** and type **p** for Page). Then type **f** for Footer (or **h** for header, if you're editing a header).
2. Choose **Footer A** or **B**, or **Header A** or **B**, depending on the one you want to edit.
3. Type **e** for Edit, and you'll see the text of your header or footer.
4. After you've changed it to what you want, press **F7** twice to return to the document.

You may also change the font, the type size, and use italics and bodface in a header or footer. Changing fonts is explained in the next lesson.

◆ *Lesson* ◆

24
Using Fonts

Although the characters you see on your screen always look pretty much the same, you can change the font in your printed document. A *font* is the complete assortment of type of one design and size. All printers, even the simplest dot matrix printers, have at least one font built into them. That font usually is Courier, which looks like what a typewriter produces; in fact, you'll sometimes hear it called typewriter face.

But you've got an expensive computer and a great word processing program, so why create documents that look like you typed them on a typewriter? Let's change fonts.

Fonts

The fonts available to you depend on your particular printer. For some printers it's possible to buy and install additional fonts. Figure 24.1 shows a sample.

Courier

Avant Garde

Palatino

Times

Helvetica

New Century Schoolbook

Bookman

Figure 24.1   A font sampler

 Be aware that you won't see the effects of different fonts on the screen. As with other WordPerfect features, you must use the View Document feature or print the document to see them. This is one area where WordPerfect for DOS is very different from WordPerfect for Windows, which does show different fonts on-screen.

Font Sizes

Fonts are usually measured in *points.* A point is 1/72 of an inch. That's sort of hard to visualize, but think of it this way: the text you read in books, like this one, is usually printed in 10, 11, or 12 point type. The bigger the point size, the larger the text.

Some printers, such as dot matrix printers, don't use the point system for measuring fonts; they use *cpi*, for characters per inch, instead. In this system, the larger the number, the *smaller* the text; therefore, 12 characters per inch is a smaller text than 10 characters per inch. Usually you'll use 10 cpi or 12 cpi for text if you have a dot-matrix printer.

The Base Font

When your printer was installed, WordPerfect selected a *base font* for it, the font that all your documents will be printed in unless you change it. Your base font is probably Courier or its equivalent; it may be called Pica or Elite. You're not stuck with your base font, however, as you'll learn in the next section.

Changing the Base Font

To change the base font for a whole document, retrieve a document into the editing screen, and go to the beginning of it.

1. Choose **Font** from the Font menu or press **Ctrl-F8** and type **f** for Base Font. You'll see all the fonts available on your printer. (Figure 24.2 shows a typical list for a PostScript printer, and Figure 24.3 shows fonts for a dot-matrix printer. You may see a completely different list, depending on which printer you have.)

2. To switch to a different font, use the arrow keys to move to the font you want. When it's highlighted, press **Enter**.

```
Base Font
 Helvetica Oblique
 ITC Avant Garde Gothic Book
 ITC Avant Garde Gothic Book Oblique
 ITC Avant Garde Gothic Demi
 ITC Avant Garde Gothic Demi Oblique
 ITC Bookman Demi
 ITC Bookman Demi Italic
 ITC Bookman Light
 ITC Bookman Light Italic
 ITC Zapf Chancery Medium Italic
 ITC Zapf Dingbats
 New Century Schoolbook
 New Century Schoolbook Bold
 New Century Schoolbook Bold Italic
 New Century Schoolbook Italic
 Palatino
 Palatino Bold
 Palatino Bold Italic
 Palatino Italic
 Symbol
* Times Roman
 Select; N Name search:
```

Figure 24.2 PostScript fonts

3. Your printer may ask you for a point size, or you
    may choose the font size as you choose the font,
    depending on which kind of printer you have. If
    you're asked for a point size, the program will
    suggest one. You can press Enter to accept its
    recommendation, or type **10** or **12** (for regular
    text) and press **Enter**.

```
Base Font
 Elite
 Elite Condensed
 Elite Condensed Italic
 Elite Dbl-Wide
 Elite Dbl-Wide Italic
 Elite Italic
* Pica
 Pica Condensed
 Pica Condensed Dbl-Wide
 Pica Condensed Dbl-Wide Italic
 Pica Condensed Italic
 Pica Dbl-Wide
 Pica Dbl-Wide Italic
 Pica Italic
 Proportional
 Proportional Italic



 Select; N Name search:
```

Figure 24.3 Dot matrix printer fonts

4. Now you've changed the font for the whole document. Press **Shift-F7** and type **v** for View Document to see the results.

⇨ **Note:** Even in the View Document screen, you won't see the *actual* font represented. WordPerfect uses three different screen fonts to approximate the fonts output on a printed document. Therefore, you'll need to print the document to see the actual font.

More than One Font in a Document

Often you'll want to use different fonts to accent or highlight separate sections of a document—for headings, for example. This is easy to do. All you have to remember is that WordPerfect changes the font beginning at the current cursor position. You first put the cursor where you want the font to change, make the change, and then move to the place where you want to revert to regular text and switch back to the base font, or still another font. Let's try this.

1. Type a short heading, such as **December Report**.
2. Move to the *D* in *December* and choose **Base Font** from the Font menu. Select a new font and size from the list that's available to you.
3. Move to just after the *t* in *Report*. This time, use the keyboard shortcut **Shift-F8** and type **n** for Normal.
4. To check the results, use **View Document**.

Good Design

Once you discover how easy it is to switch fonts in a document, you may be tempted to use as many fonts as your printer can produce. This doesn't create a good design, however. It's best to use only one font for text and another one or at most two for headings within a single document. If you use too many fonts in a document, it will look confusing and be hard to read. Follow these simple guidelines to keep your documents looking professionally designed:

- Use a *serif font* (one that has little strokes at the ends of the letters) for text, like the text in this book. Times Roman is an example of a serif font.
- Use a *sans serif font* (one without the little strokes on the letters) for headings, like the headings you see here. Helvetica is a sans serif font.
- Make body text no larger than 12 points and no smaller than 10 points, so it will be easy to read (10 cpi or 12 cpi on a dot matrix printer).
- Make headings slightly larger than text, but not too large. If you're using 12-point text, use 14 or 16 point type for headings.
- For variety *within a font*, you can switch to *italics* and **boldface**, as you'll see in the next lesson.

25

Changing Font Attributes

WordPerfect calls the special characteristics of a particular font its *attributes*, most of which you're already familiar with. Attributes include:

- Boldface
- Italics
- Underline
- Double underline
- Outline
- Shadow
- Small caps
- Redline
- Strikeout

Figure 25.1 shows how most of these attributes look in a printed document.

| **Boldface** | *Italics* | ~~Strikeout~~ |
| Double underline | | SMALL CAPS |

Figure 25.1   Different text attributes

 Tip
Not all printers can produce all these special effects. To see which of them your printer can handle, retrieve the PRINTER.TST document that comes with WordPerfect and print it. This test document will show whether your printer can print superscripts, subscripts, underlining, redline, and strikeout. It also contains a graphic image, a sample equation, a table, a footnote, and more, so you can see how your printer handles graphics, too.

It's easy to incorporate these different attributes (or appearances) in a document. They all can be accessed from the Font menu (you'll have to choose Appearance to get some of them); in addition there are quick keyboard shortcuts for boldfacing and underlining text.

Boldfacing Text

The quickest way to make text **boldface** as you're typing it is to press **F6**. You can also choose **Appearance** from the Font menu and then select **Bold**. To resume regular text, press **F6** again, or choose **Normal** from the Font menu.

Underlining Text

To underline text as you're typing it, press **F8**, or choose **Appearance** from the Font menu and then select **Undln**. To resume regular text, press **F8** again, or choose **Normal** from the Font menu.

Italicizing Text

To *italicize* text as you're typing it, the procedure is a little different, because there's no key assigned to it. Choose **Appearance** from the Font menu and then choose **Italc**. The keyboard shortcut is to press **Ctrl-F8**, type **a** for Appearance and **i** for Italics.

Tip
The keyboard shortcut, Ctrl-F8 a, reveals all nine attribute choices in one line, so it's easy to pick the one you want.

To return to normal text, choose **Normal** from the Font menu or press **Ctrl-F8** and type **n** for Normal.

Superscripts and Subscripts

To create a subscript or a superscript in text as you're typing it, the procedure again is a little different:

1. Choose **Superscript** or **Subscript** from the Font menu. The keyboard shortcut is **Ctrl-F8**, type **s** for Size and **p** (for Superscript) or **b** (for Subscript).
2. Type the character you want to be raised (super-script) or lowered (subscript).

3. To return to regular text, choose **Normal** from the Font menu or press **Ctrl-F8** and type **n** for Normal.

Tip

If you want to change the size or appearance of only a few characters, words, or lines of text, mark them as a block and then make the change. It's usually faster than changing attributes as you type.

◆ *Lesson* ◆

26
Keeping Text Together

One of the most often asked questions when learning WordPerfect is, "How do I make one page end and start a new page?" Well, WordPerfect automatically paginates documents for you, but there will be times when you want to force a page to break at a specific place. When you do, just press **Ctrl-Enter**.

Page Breaks

Even if you don't have a very big document on the screen right now—or any document at all, for that matter—you can try this to see how it works. Then you'll know how to use this feature when you create longer documents.

1. Press **Ctrl-Enter**. A double-dash line will appear across the width of screen (Figure 26.1), which indicates a page break. When your document is

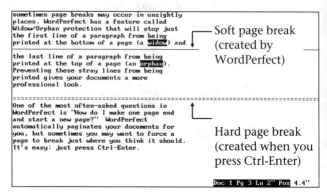

sometimes page breaks may occur in unsightly
places. WordPerfect has a feature called
Widow/Orphan protection that will stop just
the first line of a paragraph from being
printed at the bottom of a page (a `widow`) and

the last line of a paragraph from being
printed at the top of a page (an `orphan`).
Preventing these stray lines from being
printed gives your documents a more
professional look.

One of the most often-asked questions in
WordPerfect is 'How do I make one page end
and start a new page?' WordPerfect
automatically paginates your documents for
you, but sometimes you may want to force a
page to break just where you think it should.
It's easy: just press Ctrl-Enter.

—— Soft page break
(created by
WordPerfect)

Hard page break
(created when you
press Ctrl-Enter)

Doc 1 Pg 3 Ln 2" Pos 4.4"

Figure 26.1　Forcing a page break

    printed, the page will end at that line and a new
    page will begin with the first line of text that
    appears below the dashed line.

2. Press **Backspace** to delete the page break.

Other Built-In Features

WordPerfect has three other features that you can use
when you want control over page breaks, instead of
letting WordPerfect make those choices. They are:

- Widow/Orphan Protection
- Block Protection
- Conditional End of Page

Widows and Orphans

Even with the program's automatic pagination capabil-
ity, page breaks will occur in unsightly places. To

prevent this, WordPerfect has a feature called Widow/Orphan Protection that, when turned on, prohibits a single word or line of a paragraph from printing at the bottom of a page (a *widow*) and the last word or line of a paragraph from printing at the top of a page (an *orphan*). Using this feature will give your documents a more cohesive look.

To turn on Widow/Orphan Protection for the whole document:

1. Move to the beginning of the document (**Home Home Up arrow**).
2. Select **Line** from the Layout menu (or press **Shift-F8** and type **l** for Line).
3. Type **w** for Widow/Orphan Protection; then type **y** for Yes.
4. Press **F7** to return to the document.

Block Protection

WordPerfect's Block Protection feature ensures that all of a table or chart stays on one page. Here's how to use this feature:

1. First, mark as a block the text you don't want broken between pages. Press **Alt-F4**, or select **Block** from the Edit menu.
2. Use the arrow keys to highlight the text, or drag over it with the mouse to mark it.
3. Choose **Protect Block** from the Edit menu or press **Shift-F8**.
4. If you press **Shift-F8**, you'll see a "Protect block?" prompt. Type **y** for Yes.

Now, if WordPerfect has to break the page near that text and it won't fit on the current page, it will skip to the next page and then print the text you protected.

Conditional End of Page

If what you want to do is keep a few lines of text together with a heading that precedes them, you use the feature called Conditional End of Page.

1. First, count the lines you want to stay together; count any blank lines that are between text lines, as well.
2. Move the cursor to the line *above* the lines you want to stay on one page.
3. Choose **Other** from the Layout menu, or press **Shift-F8** and type **o** for Other.
4. Type **c** for Conditional End of Page.
5. Enter the number of lines you counted and press **Enter**.
6. Press **F7** to return to your document.

27

Working with Columns

If you write newsletters or create flyers, you will want to know how to arrange text in columns. WordPerfect lets you create two kinds of text columns:

Newspaper columns	Text flows from the bottom of one column to the top of the next column, like in a newspaper as shown in Figure 27.1.
Parallel columns	Two or more columns of text that must align horizontally are spaced appropriately (Figure 27.2).

Creating Newspaper Columns

Most of the time, you'll probably use newspaper columns for text in newsletters and such. Here's how to create them the easy way.

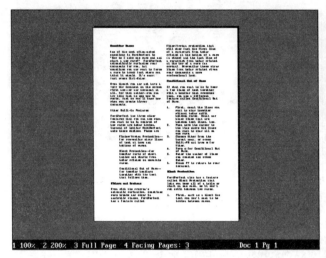

Figure 27.1 Newspaper columns

1. Type the text you want to put into columns.
2. Move to the beginning of the location where you want the columns to appear. Then choose **Define** from the Layout menu (or press **Alt-F7** and type **c** for Columns and **d** for Define).

   You must define columns before you can turn them on, or WordPerfect won't know what kind of columns you want, and will respond with an error message.

3. You'll see the screen in Figure 27.3. If you want two equally spaced columns, press **F7** to exit from this screen. If you want a different number of columns such as 3 or 4, type that number.

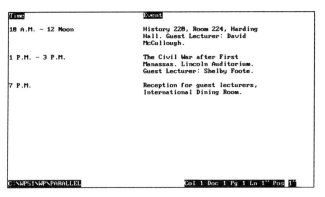

Time	Event
10 A.M. – 12 Noon	History 220, Room 224, Harding Hall. Guest Lecturer: David McCullough.
1 P.M. – 3 P.M.	The Civil War after First Manassas. Lincoln Auditorium. Guest Lecturer: Shelby Foote.
7 P.M.	Reception for guest lecturers, International Dining Room.

C:\WP51\WP\PARALLEL   Col 1 Doc 1 Pg 1 Ln 1" Pos 1"

Figure 27.2 Parallel columns

WordPerfect automatically figures out the spacing between the columns. You can change the distance between the columns if you want columns that aren't the same size.

4. When you've chosen how many columns you want, press **F7** to exit.

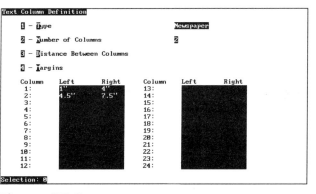

Text Column Definition

    1 – Type   Newspaper
    2 – Number of Columns   2
    3 – Distance Between Columns
    4 – Margins

    Column   Left   Right   Column   Left   Right
      1:     1"   4"   13:
      2:     4.5"   7.5"   14:
      3:                           15:
      4:                           16:
      5:                           17:
      6:                           18:
      7:                           19:
      8:                           20:
      9:                           21:
     10:                           22:
     11:                           23:
     12:                           24:

Selection: 0

Figure 27.3 Column Definition screen

5. Turn on columns by typing **o** for On. Word-Perfect automatically arranges the text in columns for you. To force a column to end at a certain point, put the cursor at that location and press **Ctrl-Enter**.

6. Move the cursor to the end of the text you want to be in columns. Choose **Columns** from the Layout menu (or press **Alt-F7** and type **c**); then type **f** for Off.

Tip
You can define columns at the beginning of a document and turn them off and on throughout the document, so that text appears in columns in different places. WordPerfect uses the original column definition you set up until you define another one.

Parallel Columns

Parallel columns are used for things like scripts and agendas, where one column of text must align with another.

To define parallel columns, simply type **t** for Type at the Column Definition screen (Figure 27.3) and then type **p** for Parallel Columns, or **b** for parallel columns with Block Protect, which means that columns won't be broken at the ends of pages.

After you've defined parallel columns and turned them on, move the cursor to *each* place that you want a column to end and a new one to begin and press **Ctrl-Enter**.

Editing text in parallel columns can be difficult because the alignment will change. If you need to create parallel columns, consider using WordPerfect's Tables feature instead. It's much easier to edit text in cells, and you can remove the lines from the table so that they won't be printed in your document and nobody will know that it's a table.

◆ *Lesson* ◆

28

Working with Reveal Codes

As you create and format documents, WordPerfect inserts invisible codes behind the scenes. We've already talked about some of them. These codes indicate where you pressed Enter for a hard return, for example, or where you pressed Tab to indent text. Most of the time these codes are best left unseen as they go about their business and you go about yours. But there will be occasions when no matter how you format a page, nothing happens—the previous formatting stays in position. That's when it's time to open the Reveal Codes window to see what's going on.

Revealing Codes

To view the codes that are formatting your document behind the scenes, choose **Reveal Codes** from the Edit menu or press **Alt-F3**. The screen will split, and at the lower half of the screen you'll see a duplicate of the text, but with the codes visible.

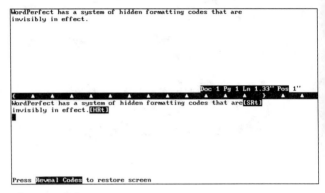

Figure 28.1   Viewing hard and soft returns

As you move the cursor through your document at the top half of the screen, you'll notice that the cursor moves in the lower window simultaneously.

Try this now. Clear the screen first, then:

1. Type this sentence: **WordPerfect has a system of hidden formatting codes that are invisibly in effect.** Press **Enter**.

2. Choose **Reveal Codes** from the Edit menu or press **Alt-F3**. The screen will split to show the sentence you just typed, followed by the hard return [HRt] code that indicates where you pressed Enter (Figure 28.1).

3. You'll also see a [SRt] code at the end of each line. This is a *soft return*, which indicates where the program automatically wrapped text to the next line. If you enter new words in the sentence you already typed, the lines will break differently. Hard returns don't change—they stay where you put them.

4. Next press **F6** and type **bold**. Then press **F6** again. Now the screen shows the word *bold* enclosed in the codes [BOLD] and [bold]. The first code turns on boldfacing, and the last code turns it off.

5. Move the cursor to either one of the bold codes and delete it. The boldfacing disappears from your document.

6. Press **Alt-F3** to close the Reveal Codes window.

Troubleshooting with Reveal Codes

When formatting problems force you to invoke Reveal Codes, you'll probably discover that you are the culprit: you may have mistakenly pressed a key that inserted a code you didn't want, or left one in from previous editing. So it's good to know how to check the codes and understand what they look like and how they are being used.

 A common error is to press Shift-F6 by mistake, which centers text; if you do this when you don't intend to, you may see text disappear from the screen. Or, if numbers and letters start mysteriously appearing whenever you press Enter, you may have turned outlining on.

Common Codes

WordPerfect has cryptic codes for all of its formatting commands, and most of the time you won't have to worry about them. Nevertheless, it's a good idea to familiarize yourself with them and what they do. As you can see, most of them are easy to understand just by looking at their names:

[HRt]	Hard return (inserted when you press Enter)
[SRt]	Soft return (inserted by the program as it wraps lines)
[DSRt]	Deletable soft return (also inserted by the program)
[HPg]	Hard page break (inserted by you)
[SPg]	Soft page break (inserted by the program as it paginates)
[BOLD][bold]	Boldface
[ITAL][ital]	Italics
[Ln Spacing:]	Line spacing
[L/R Mar:]	Left and right margins
[T/B Mar:]	Top and bottom margins
[-]	Hyphen
[Tab]	Tab
[DEC TAB]	Decimal tab
[Cntr Tab]	Centered tab
[Just:]	Justification (Left, Right, Full, or Center)
[Center]	Centered text
[->Indent]	Indent

[->Indent<-]	Double indent
[Font:]	Font change
[Footer:], **[Header:]**	Footers and headers
[Outline On]	Outlining

Searching for Codes

As you move through your document, you'll see the codes that format it. But in a long document, viewing each page to locate a particular code can take a while. That's why WordPerfect lets you search for formatting codes, in the same way that you search for text.

1. Go to the beginning of the document, or to the place where you think the format code might be. Be sure to place the cursor *above* where you think the code may be if you're searching forward!
2. Press **F2** or choose **Forward** from the Search menu. (Shift-F2 lets you search backward.)
3. Then, instead of entering text to search for, press the keys that create the code you're hunting for. For example, to search for a [Center] code, press **Shift-F6**. To search for a [BOLD] code, press **F6**.
4. Press **F2** again to start the search. WordPerfect will locate the next occurrence of that code, and you can open the Reveal Codes window to see it.

Sometimes you may have to press more than one key to generate a code. For example, if you're searching for the place in the document where you changed justification, you'd need to press **Shift-F8** and type **l** for Line and **j** for justification.

You can't use the menus to generate the codes
at the Search prompt. You must press the keys
that generate the codes. If you're not sure what
they are, press F3 for Help and type the letter of
the feature you want to search for, such as C for
Center. The Help screen will list the keys you
need to press for that feature.

Tip

You can use the search and replace feature to
remove codes, too. For example, to remove all
the boldfacing from a document, press Alt-F2
(Replace), type n for No, and press F6 to search
for [BOLD] codes. At the "Replace with:"
prompt, press F2 to replace them with nothing
(remove them from the document). You'll be
asked to confirm that this is what you want.

29

Being Creative with WordPerfect

WordPerfect has many more features than we've touched on in these short lessons, including:

- Automatic references
- Customized keyboards
- Equations
- File management
- Foreign language typing
- Graphics
- Macros
- Mail merge
- Master documents
- Outlines
- Reference aids
- Sorting and selecting
- Special symbols
- Spreadsheets
- Styles
- Tables
- Thesaurus

Where do you begin? First of all, remember, you don't need to learn any more features right now unless you need them. The skills you mastered in the lessons in this book are enough to get you through most situations. Later, if you need to do a mail merge, say, or type equations, you can find out more about them by using some of the other sources listed in the Epilogue, or by checking out the on-line Help in WordPerfect.

And don't try to learn everything at once, because WordPerfect is incredibly rich in features. Discover how to use one feature at a time.

Setting Up WordPerfect the Way You Want It

As you've worked through the exercises in these lessons, you may have decided a few things about how you'd like the program to always operate for you. For example, you may want to use left justification in all your documents, have page numbers on all printed pages, or pick a new base font for all the documents you create.

Tip
Changing the screen colors is fun if you have a color monitor. You can make the Doc 1 window one color and the Doc 2 window another color to be able to see at a glance which one you're in, for example.

WordPerfect has a Setup menu that lets you specify exactly how you want certain features to operate. When you get a chance, explore the Setup menus (Setup is on the File menu) and see all the things you can change.

Changing Initial Codes

Most of the setup menus are easy to understand, but Initial Codes can be a little confusing. Initial codes are the formatting codes that you want to be in effect in *every* document you create. Say, for example, that you want double spacing in all your documents. Instead of changing the line spacing each time you start a new document, just put the code for double spacing in the Initial Codes window. Here's how to do it.

1. Choose **Setup** from the File menu; then choose **Initial Settings**. (**Shift-F1** is the shortcut to the Setup menus.)
2. Choose **Initial Codes**.
3. Do what you'd normally do to format a document. You'll see the codes appear as you press the keys that generate them. (Remember, you can press **F3** for Help if you've forgotten which keys to use.) For example, to turn on double spacing, press **Shift-F8**, type **l** for Line and **s** for Spacing and enter **2**. To turn on left justification, press **Shift-F8** and type **l j l** and press **Enter**.
4. When you've entered all the formatting codes you want to be in effect in all your documents, press **F7** until you exit from the Setup menus and return to your document.

Initial codes do *not* show up in your Reveal Codes screen, although they'll be in effect in all the documents you create from now on. If you're having trouble formatting a document and you've set initial codes, go back to the Setup menus and see which settings you've changed.

The Next Step: Macros?

Before you go much further with WordPerfect, it's a good idea to explore how to use its macro recorder. Macros are easy, because the program faithfully records everything you do until you turn the macro recorder off. If you make a mistake, just correct it, and the program records the keystrokes that correct it. So you can have it automatically type text for you—to set up your return address, for instance. You can have macros automate any repetitive keystrokes you make all the time, like **F10 Enter y** to save a document as you're working on it. It's much easier to type Alt-S for Save!

Sneak Preview: How to Record a Macro

It's easy to record a macro:

1. Choose **Macro** from the Tools menu and then choose **Define**, or press **Ctrl-F10**.
2. Give your macro a name, such as Alt-S (press **Alt** and **s**) or Save. If you like, enter a description of what it does.

3. Type the keystrokes the macro is to carry out. You can type from the keyboard or choose from the pull-down menus to carry out sequences of commands.

4. Turn off the macro recorder by pressing **Ctrl-F10**, or choosing **Macro** from the Tools menu and selecting **Define** again.

Then, to execute the macro any time you want to use it, type the Alt key sequence you assigned it to. If you gave it a name instead, press **Alt-F10**, enter the name, and press **Enter**. You can choose Macro from the Tools menu, then choose Execute, enter the name, and press Enter, too. That's it. Whatever you recorded will be repeated.

When I first learned WordPerfect, I recorded three macros: Alt-C for Copy (to copy highlighted text), Alt-X for Cut (so that I didn't have to always type that y for Yes every time I deleted text), and Alt-S for Save. You'll be amazed how easy it is to record these three little macros and how much more convenient the program will become when they are put to use.

Epilogue
Where to Go from Here

Now that you've finished this book, you're ready to start exploring WordPerfect on your own. A variety of sources are available for more information on WordPerfect and its advanced features.

Magazines

WordPerfect Magazine
(801) 228-9626
270 West Center Street
Orem, UT 84057

WordPerfect Technical Support

Installation	(800) 533-9605
Features	(800) 541-5096
Printers	(800) 541-5097
Deaf support-TDD	(800) 321-3256
After hours number	
(not toll free)	(801) 222-9010

CompuServe Forums

WordPerfect Support on CompuServe
GO WPSG

Books

WordPerfect 5.1 Macros and Templates
by Gordon McComb

Mastering WordPerfect 5.1
by Alan Simpson

Index